HISTORY

SERIES TITLES

PREHISTORY	I	XIII	SETTLING THE AMERICAS
MESOPOTAMIA AND THE BIBLE LANDS	II	XIV	ASIAN AND AFRICAN EMPIRES
ANCIENT EGYPT AND GREECE	III	XV	THE INDUSTRIAL REVOLUTION
THE ROMAN WORLD	IV	XVI	ENLIGHTENMENT AND REVOLUTION
ASIAN CIVILIZATIONS	V	XVII	NATIONALISM AND THE ROMANTIC MOVEMENT
AMERICAS AND THE PACIFIC	VI	XVIII	THE AGE OF EMPIRE
EARLY MEDIEVAL TIMES	VII	XIX	NORTH AMERICA: EXPANSION, CIVIL WAR, AND EMERGENCE
BEYOND EUROPE	VIII	XX	TURN OF THE CENTURY AND THE GREAT WAR
LATE MEDIEVAL EUROPE	IX	XXI	VERSAILLES TO WORLD WAR II
RENAISSANCE EUROPE	X	XXII	1945 TO THE COLD WAR
VOYAGES OF DISCOVERY	XI	XXIII	1991 TO THE 21ST CENTURY
BIRTH OF MODERN NATIONS	XII	XXIV	ISSUES TODAY

VERSAILLES TO WORLD WAR II
was created and produced by McRae Books Srl
Via del Salviatino, 1 – 50016 Florence (Italy)
info@mcraebooks.com
www.mcraebooks.com

Publishers: Anne McRae, Marco Nardi
Art Director: Marco Nardi
Series Editor: Anne McRae
Author: Neil Morris
Layouts: Nick Leggett, Starry Dog Books Ltd
Title Editor: Vicky Egan
Project Editor: Loredana Agosta
Research: Vicky Egan
Repro: Litocolor, Florence

Main Illustrations: Leonello Calvetti 11, Lorenzo Cecchi 36-37,
Francesca D'Ottavi 3, 13, 15, 26-27, 42-43, Andrea Ricciardi di
Gaudesi 45

Illustrations: Lorenzo Cecchi, MM Comunicazione
(Manuela Cappon, Monica Favilli, Gianni Sbragi, Cecilia Scutti),
Paola Ravaglia, Studio Stalio (Alessandro Cantucci, Fabiano
Fabbrucci, Margherita Salvadori)

Maps: M. Paola Baldanzi

Photos: THE BRIDGEMAN ART LIBRARY: 6bl, 7tl, 7tr, 8bc, 10cl, 11bl,
14ar, 14cr, 18ar, 22cl, 29 cr, 32bl, 33 br, 41al, 45ar; © Antonio
Petrucelli/ Bibliotheque des Arts Décoratifs, Paris / Archives
Charmet / The Bridgeman Art Library 12al; © British Library Board
/ The Bridgeman Art Library 10cr; © Dorothea Lange / Library of
Congress, Washington D.C., USA / The Bridgeman Art Library
15al; © Fontsere / Private Collection / Archives Charmet / The
Bridgeman Art Library 30cl; © Gignoux / Private Collection /
Archives Charmet / The Bridgeman Art Library 20bl; © John Held
Junior, Collection of the New-York Historical Society, USA / The
Bridgeman Art Library 8-9l; © Pablo Picasso by SIAE 2009 /
Museo Nacional Centro de Arte Reina Sofia, Madrid, Spain / The
Bridgeman Art Library 30-31ac; © Paul Maeyaert / The Bridgeman
Art Library 6-7b; © R. Vepkhvadze / Bibliotheque des Arts
Décoratifs, Paris, France / Archives Charmet / The Bridgeman Art
Library 20ar; © Royal Mail Group Ltd. / The Bridgeman Art
Library 39ar, Ethel Gabain / Private Collection / The Bridgeman
Art Library 45al; © Salvador Dalí by SIAE 2009 / Museum of
Modern Art, New York, USA/ The Bridgeman Art Library 44ar; ©
Wang Sheng Lie / Private Collection / Archives Charmet / The
Bridgeman Art Library 28-29; © Y. Romas / Private Collection /
RIA Novosti / The Bridgeman Art Library 20-21c. CTESIPHON
BOOKS: 24-25b. GETTY IMAGES: 22ad; Imagno/Getty Images 34ad;
Keystone Features/Getty Images 38cl, 42cl; Popperfoto/Getty
Images 40c; Reg Speller/Fox Photos/Getty Images 38-39b. THE ART
ARCHIVE: The Art Archive / Alfredo Dagli Orti 23; The Art Archive /
Central Bank Teheran / Gianni Dagli Orti 24cr; The Art Archive /
Domenica del Corriere / Gianni Dagli Orti 40bl; The Art Archive /
Eileen Tweedy 26c; The Art Archive / John Meek 27cb, 34-35,
38cr; The Art Archive: The Art Archive / Culver Pictures 7b, 18-
19c. SCIENCE MUSEUM/SSPL: 10bs. THE KOBAL COLLECTION: 20th
Century Fox / The Kobal Collection 14bc, RKO / The Kobal
Collection / Longet, Gaston 16-17c; RKO / The Kobal Collection
17bs; Touchstone/Jerry Bruckmeyer Inc / The Kobal Collection /
Cooper, Andrew 40-41b; Walt Disney / The Kobal Collection 16cs;
Warner Bros / The Kobal Collection 16ar. LONELY PLANET IMAGES:
Jonathan Smith / Lonely Planet Images 19al, 19c.

Consultant: Professor Hew Strachan,
Chichele Professor of the History of War,
All Souls College, Oxford, UK

From Versailles to the End of World War Two
 ISBN 9788860981837

2009923565

Printed and bound in Malaysia.

HIST☉RY

Versailles to World War II

Neil Morris

Consultant:
Professor Hew Strachan,
Chichele Professor of the History of War,
All Souls College, Oxford, UK

Zak
BOOKS

Contents

5 Introduction

6 Versailles to World War II

8 America: the Roaring Twenties

10 The Transportation Revolution

12 The Great Depression

14 A New Deal for the USA

16 The Hollywood Dream Factory

18 Birth of the Soviet Union

20 Stalin's Russia

22 Fascism in Italy

24 Reshaping the Middle East

26 Britain's Imperial Sunset

28 China in Turmoil

30 Civil War in Spain

32 Hitler's Rise to Power

34 World War II Breaks Out

36 Hitler's War to the West and East

38 Britain's Home Front

40 Battle For the Pacific

42 Path to Victory

44 Arts and Science

46 Glossary

47 Index

Two fascist leaders: Il Duce (Mussolini) and Der Führer (Hitler).

TIMELINE

	1918	1921	1924	1927
THE UNITED STATES	First air-mail service between the US and Canada. Women in the US are given the right to vote.	Rudolph Valentino becomes a star in *The Four Horsemen of the Apocalypse*. The Charleston and marathon dancing become national crazes.	NBC (the National Broadcasting Company) is formed.	New York Stock Exchange crashes. The first Oscars (left) are awarded.
THE SOVIET UNION	The Russian capital moves from Petrograd back to Moscow.	Mass famine begins. Stalin becomes General Secretary of the Communist Party.	Death of Vladimir Ilyich Lenin. Beginning of a power struggle between Stalin and Trotsky (left) for control of the Soviet state.	
ITALY AND SPAIN		In Italy, Mussolini founds the Fascist Combat group.	In Italy, secret police and political courts are established.	
THE MIDDLE EAST	Famine devastates northern Persia. Britain takes control of Palestine.	The Qajar government of Persia is overthrown. Kemal Atatürk is elected president of the new republic of Turkey.	Secular law replaces religious law in Turkey.	Huge oil fields are discovered near Kirkuk, Iraq, bringing economic improvement.
GREAT BRITAIN	Irish Republicans declare Ireland independent.	The Bloomsbury Group, including Virginia Woolf (left), begin to exercise wide influence. Civil war in Ireland, 1922–23.		
CHINA	Mao Zeroing learns about Communism.	Sun Yat-sen reorganizes the Nationalist Party and Army with help from the Soviet Union. Peasants endure hunger, hardship and high taxes.		
WORLD WAR II		Hitler's political career begins when he takes over the National Socialist German Workers' Party.	The Allies remove their occupational troops from the Ruhr in Germany. At the Locarno Conference, treaties are signed guaranteeing peace in Europe.	Germany's leader, Gustav Stresemann, dies.

Introduction

At the end of the Great War in 1918, many people felt there was going to be a new, peaceful world order. However, the fun times of the roaring twenties were quickly followed by a worldwide economic crisis. At the same time, Italy fell under the grip of fascism and Stalin's brand of communism gained control of the Soviet Union. In Germany, where many people felt they had been treated too harshly by the 1919 peace settlement, Hitler promised to build a powerful new empire. The Nazi dictator's imperialist plans led directly to the outbreak of another disastrous world war. This book tells the story of the interwar period, from the Treaty of Versailles to the German invasion of Poland. It also covers the events of the Second World War itself, from its beginning to the dropping of atomic bombs on Japan that brought it to a close.

Londoners celebrate the end of the Great War.

The atomic bombs dropped on Japan in 1945 spread lethal radiation over a wide area.

1930	1933	1936	1939	1942

A quarter of the US population is unemployed.

Roosevelt introduces his New Deal reforms to help lift the economic depression.

Roosevelt wins re-election.

Millionaire pilot Howard Hughes sets a transcontinental flight record.

Roosevelt becomes the first US president to appear on television, as he opens the World's Fair in New York.

The American fleet at Pearl Harbor is attacked by Japan.

Millions of Russians die of famine 1932–33.

Stalin's "purge" trials eliminate thousands of political opponents and army generals.

Trotsky founds the Fourth International (1938) in opposition to Stalin.

The Soviet Union joins the war against Germany, its former ally, when Hitler invades.

Fascist dictator of Italy, Benito Mussolini, invades Abyssinia.

Franco becomes chief of the Spanish army's general staff.

Mussolini forms an alliance –the Pact of Steel–with Hitler in May 1939.

Franco's dictatorship starts (lasts until 1975).

Iraq gains independence after the British mandate officially ends, 1932.

Saudi Arabia gains independence.

Arabs revolt against British rule in Palestine (first "intimated").

Oil is discovered in Saudi Arabia by an American company.

1941, Reza Shah Pahlevi ascends to the throne of Iran when his father is deposed by British and Soviet troops for collaborating with the Nazis.

The Statute of Westminster establishes the Commonwealth of Nations, 1931.

In January 1934, the British Union of Fascists (BUF) holds a rally attended by more than 10,000 supporters.

In January, King George V dies. Edward succeeds him as king. In December, Edward VIII abdicates.

Sir Frank Whittle invents the Jet Engine in 1937.

George VI is the first British monarch to visit the USA.

George VI institutes the George Cross and George Medal for acts of bravery by civilians.

The Chinese Communist Party confirms Mao Zeroing in the new post of chairman.

Beginning of the Sino–Japanese War, causing a second United Front of Chinese forces; the Soviet Union and China sign a non-aggression pact.

Hitler becomes Chancellor of Germany.

Germany leaves the League of Nations.

Hitler introduces conscription.

Germany rearms and occupies the Rhineland.

Hitler outlines secret plans to conquer Austria and Czechoslovakia.

Britain and France pledge to declare war against Germany if Hitler invades Poland.

War is declared 3rd September 1939.

Tanks and other military equipment were systematically destroyed after the war.

Versailles to World War II

People thought the 1914–18 conflict was the "war to end all wars." Millions had died, and the victors saw an opportunity to create a new world order. Yet just 21 years later, the world was at war again. Many problems of the interwar years helped cause this. They included failings in the peace settlement, a global economic crisis and great splits between fascists, communists and capitalists.

Treaty of Versailles

The treaty set out the terms of peace between the Allied Powers and Germany. The German representatives were required to sign it without negotiation and with the threat that the war would resume if they did not. The main provisions disarmed Germany, revised European boundaries and called for reparations (compensation payments) from Germany, which was declared solely responsible for the war. These terms were seen as too lenient by the French and others.

The last lines of the treaty, signed by the "Big Four"—Woodrow Wilson (USA), David Lloyd George (UK), Georges Clemenceau (France) and Vittorio Orlando (Italy).

The German Military Cemetery at Vladslo, Belgium. Many German survivors felt that the war had swept away the finest of a whole generation.

The treaty was signed in the Palace of Versailles, the 17th-century former French royal residence just outside Paris. The US Senate never ratified (accepted) the treaty.

The Prince of Wales (later Edward VIII, see page 27) toured parts of the British Empire in 1930.

Colonial Changes

Post-war treaties altered the balance of power in European overseas colonies. Under the Treaty of Versailles, Germany lost its foreign territories. With the agreement of the League of Nations, but without consulting any local people, Britain was given control of German East Africa and France gained most of the Cameroons. Germany's Pacific colonies were divided between Japan, Australia and New Zealand. Britain and France also gained mandated territories in the Middle East from the defeated Ottoman Empire (see page 24).

League of Nations

The Paris Peace Conference established the League of Nations in January 1920, with headquarters in Geneva, Switzerland. The League acted as a peacekeeping agency, based on the principle of collective security—each member state agreed to help defend any other member attacked by another country. It also controlled specialist agencies, such as the Court of International Justice and the International Labor Organization. Sixteen years later, the League failed to stop the build-up to another world war (see page 34).

This caricature of the League of Nations, entitled 'The Promised Land: the United States of Europe', appeared in a Paris satirical journal in 1931.

EUROPE, 1919

LUX = LUXEMBOURG   NL = NETHERLANDS
SWZ = SWITZERLAND

Redrawing the Map

The collapse of Austria-Hungary led to the creation of new states, including Czechoslovakia and the Kingdom of Serbs, Croats and Slovenes (renamed Yugoslavia in 1929). Germany also lost territory from its homeland. Poland gained most of East Prussia, dividing Germany and creating a Polish Corridor to the Baltic Sea. France regained the provinces of Alsace and Lorraine, and coal mines in the Saar region.

The Rise of the Dictators

The first country to fall under the power of a fascist dictator was Italy. Mussolini began exercising total authority there in 1925 (see page 22). Four years later, Stalin—the "man of steel"—wielded absolute power in the Communist Soviet Union (see page 20). Hitler declared his Third Reich, with himself as Führer (Leader) in 1934 (see page 32). After a military coup two years later, Franco took over in Spain (see page 30).

Benito Mussolini and Adolf Hitler, together in Munich in 1937. They died within two days of each other in 1945.

America: the Roaring Twenties

By 1920 many Americans wanted to forget the horrors of the Great War. US politicians wanted to keep out of European affairs, and the Senate refused to approve the Treaty of Versailles or join the League of Nations. The successful economy meant a rising standard of living. Those young people who could now afford it were keen to enjoy themselves, wearing new fashions and dancing to new kinds of music. The decade became known as the Roaring Twenties.

Racial Tension

Some white Americans were opposed to black people having the vote and other civil rights. They terrorized black people and tried to scare them into not voting. The most feared group of extremist white people was the Ku Klux Klan, which by the mid-1920s had about four million members. It was responsible for bombings and lynchings. Members also turned their vicious hatred on Jews and other minority groups.

Ku Klux Klan members wore white robes and hoods to frighten black people and hide their own identity.

Prohibition

Members of the temperance movement and others believed that drinking alcohol led to increased poverty and crime in American society. They encouraged new laws prohibiting the making and selling of alcohol. But during the Prohibition period (1920–33), the laws were very difficult to enforce. People drank bootleg (illegal) liquor in bars called speakeasies, and some also made their own illegal spirits at home. Many came to think that Prohibition simply encouraged ordinary citizens to break the law.

Policemen pose beside an illegal still, used to produce alcohol such as whisky.

Gangland Crime

Prohibition led to more crime instead of less, because it gave gangsters the opportunity to control illegal alcohol. Gang leaders such as Al Capone (nicknamed "Scarface") dominated the criminal underworld in cities such as Chicago. They ran other rackets, as well as dealing in bootleg liquor, frightening people into allowing the gangsters to "protect" them. There were frequent shootouts between the rival gangs as they fought for control of gangland districts.

Bulletin #65840 Kansas State Criminal Bureau

WANTED FOR MURDER
GEORGE KELLY alias "MACHINE GUN" KELLY

By his authority, the Attorney General of the State of Indiana offers a reward of

$3000.00

for information leading to the capture of George Kelly.

DESCRIPTION	CRIMINAL RECORD
Age: 35	*Arrested* Kansas City, Mo. '32, armed robbery.
Height: 5-9	*Arrested* Joplin, Mo. '32, attempted extortion.
Weight: 185	*Arrested* Johnson City, Ka., bank holdup and shooting
Hair: brown	of law officer.
Eyes: brown	
Complexion: light	

THIS MAN IS HEAVILY ARMED AND DANGEROUS. HE WAS LAST SEEN IN COMPANY WITH JOHN DILLINGER AND OTHERS OF HIS GANG.

A wanted poster for "Machine Gun" Kelly, who was finally arrested for armed robbery and kidnapping.

FEBRUARY 18, 1926   Teaching o

The Jazz Age

During the 1920s, jazz music spread to the big US cities. New dances became all the rage, including the Charleston and the Black Bottom. Young women had their hair styled into short bobs, wore shorter dresses, and rolled their silk stockings down to their knees. They added lipstick, eye shadow, and nail polish to their look, and became known as "flappers."

This 1926 magazine cover shows a flapper teaching an "old dog" how to Charleston.

An early radio.

A jazz saxophonist.

Baseball

Radio stations began broadcasting baseball games during the 1920s, making the sport even more popular. In 1920, one of the greatest players, Babe Ruth, left the Boston Red Sox to join the New York Yankees. Fans flocked to see him at the new Yankee Stadium, and he rarely disappointed them, outscoring all the other batters. The Yankees won the World Series title in 1923, 1927, and 1928.

George Herman Ruth (1895–1948) was so successful that 1920s baseball is often called the "Babe Ruth Era."

Helping at Home

Many young women went out to work instead of being full-time housewives, and new inventions and industrial developments made life easier for them. Electric domestic appliances helped them spend less time on chores such as cleaning, washing, and cooking. Vacuum cleaners, washing machines, and electric irons saved hours of work, while refrigerators meant that women did not have to shop every day.

Wringer-mangles for drying clothes were attached to early washing machines.

AMERICA: THE ROARING TWENTIES

1920
The US 18th Amendment forbids people to make or sell intoxicating liquor; the 19th Amendment is ratified, giving US women the right to vote.

1921
Baseball legend Babe Ruth scores 177 runs in a single season (still an all-time record).

1922
Anti-Prohibition rallies are held in Chicago and other cities.

1923
The Charleston and marathon dancing become national crazes.

1925
Clarence Birdseye starts the frozen-food industry.

1926
The Radio Corporation of America forms the National Broadcasting Company (NBC), the first permanent national wireless network.

1927
Al Jolson appears in the first successful talking movie, The Jazz Singer.

1928
Walt Disney introduces Mickey Mouse in Steamboat Willie, the first animated film with sound.

1929
Capone gunmen murder rival Bugs Moran's gangsters in the so-called St. Valentine's Day Massacre.

The Transportation Revolution

After the First World War, the rising standard of living in the United States meant that many people could travel more. Improved methods of transportation—especially rail and, increasingly, road—allowed people to move around the growing cities and live further from their place of work. Air travel was fastest for longer distances, and American and European entrepreneurs were working toward linking the two sides of the Atlantic by plane.

Radio (this one dates from 1925) and new forms of transport rapidly made the world seem smaller.

On the Move

In the 1920s, travel began to influence popular culture. Songs were written about the expanding cities, including, in 1922, "Chicago" and "Way Down Yonder in New Orleans." A couple of years later, more songs celebrated the new interest in travel, such as "Alabamy Bound" and "California Here I Come." By 1932, Chicago's Midway Airport was the busiest in the world.

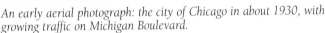

An early aerial photograph: the city of Chicago in about 1930, with growing traffic on Michigan Boulevard.

THE GREATEST BUICK EVER BUILT

Air Mail

The idea of being able to deliver mail speedily over long distances had great appeal. Air-mail deliveries had begun in 1911 in both the US and Britain, and by 1924 there were regular mail flights right across the American continent. Their speed made aircraft a popular alternative to rail transport for postal services. This helped the development of aviation and provided jobs for enthusiastic young pilots such as Charles Lindbergh (see page 11).

The letter bottom right was carried on the first non-stop transatlantic flight in 1919. British aviators John Alcock and Arthur Whitten Brown flew from Newfoundland to Ireland in a converted Vickers Vimy bomber.

This Buick advertisement appeared in 1926, when the company produced more than 260,000 cars.

Motoring On

Mass production methods in large factories meant that more motor cars could be produced and sold at cheaper prices. In 1924, the Ford Motor Company produced two million Model-T cars, and a few years later the price of a "Tin Lizzie" dropped to less than $300 (a third of its original price). There was plenty of competition for Henry Ford. While his company concentrated on affordable motoring, others such as the Buick Motor Company aimed at the luxury market.

1930s INTERCONTINENTAL AIR ROUTES

LONDON
AMSTERDAM
PARIS
TOULOUSE
NEW YORK
ALEXANDRIA
JAKARTA
SANTIAGO
CAPE TOWN
SYDNEY
PUNTA ARENAS

Pan American Transatlantic Route (1939)	Aeropostale (1930)	Imperial Airways African Route (c.1933)	KLM Amsterdam – Jakarta (1935)	Imperial Airways/ Quantas Australian Route (c.1934)

Highways in the Sky

Air routes were developed throughout the 1930s. Crossing oceans was a problem because passenger aircraft could not fly that far without re-fuelling. Flying boats offered a solution. These big planes had under-wing floats and could land and take off on water. The first transatlantic service (in 1939, see map) was flown by a Boeing 314 Clipper flying boat.

Transatlantic Solo Flight

In 1927, American aviator Charles Lindbergh made the first solo flight across the Atlantic. His long journey from New York to Paris covered 3,610 miles (5,810 km), took 33 hours and won him a prize of $25,000. People all over the world read about the feat in their newspapers, and Lindbergh became an international star. His fame helped boost the aircraft industry and made air travel more popular.

Lindbergh's plane was a Ryan high-wing monoplane, which he fitted with extra fuel tanks and named Spirit of St. Louis.

A popular celebrity, Charles Lindbergh (1902–74) was nicknamed "Lucky Lindy."

A streamlined Hudson steam locomotive powered the Empire State Express *service of the New York Central Railroad in 1938. This was a fast, efficient service.*

Railways

The US railway network covered the whole country. In the 1920s, most long-distance freight was moved by rail, and passengers also traveled by train. But the road system was improving, and cars and buses were becoming more popular. During the 1930s, the large railway companies lost money, and many went bankrupt. Those that survived did their best to attract passengers with the quality of their service, offering improved carriages, good food, and fast, powerful locomotives.

The Great Depression

During the American business boom of the 1920s, people were keen to invest and speculate on the Stock Exchange. Share prices went up and up. Some overestimated their value, and everything changed in 1929, when the New York Stock Exchange crashed. This started a huge international business slump, reaching its lowest point in 1932. As trade collapsed, millions of people lost their jobs and many struggled simply to survive.

Boom before bust. Christmas shopping in 1928.

Wealthy people who lost money tried to sell everything they could to raise cash.

Effects in the USA

For more than three years after the Stock Exchange crash of 1929, share prices kept on falling and businesses failed. Millions of Americans lost their savings, and many even lost their homes because they could not repay loans. By 1932, thousands of families were wandering the country, seeking shelter, and begging for food. Many starved or died of disease. For those who survived, life was very different from the Roaring Twenties, as their insecurity and financial worries grew.

World Trade

The US crash affected world trade, and bank and business failures led to a global economic crisis. At first Europe was worst affected, and bread lines and soup kitchens began to appear in Britain and elsewhere. Those countries that produced food and raw materials for the USA and Europe found that people could no longer afford their goods, and they too suffered.

In the United States and elsewhere, soup kitchens were set up to feed the poor and homeless.

Terrifying walls of dust created "black blizzard" dust storms in South Dakota in 1934.

The Dust Bowl

During the 1930s, severe droughts struck the southern Great Plains of the United States. As the soil dried out, crops began to fail. Prairie grasses died, and soon vast dust storms started blowing up. They damaged huge areas of Colorado, Kansas, New Mexico, Oklahoma, and Texas. The affected region came to be known as the Dust Bowl.

The Curse of Unemployment

In the US the unemployment rate reached 9 percent in 1930. Three years later roughly a quarter of the working population—13 million people—was unemployed. The situation was no better in other parts of the world. In 1932, unemployment reached 30 percent in Germany, 24 percent in Belgium, and 21 percent in Britain. Overall, in that year world unemployment rose to nearly 30 percent. To make things worse, those in work suffered pay cuts as businesses struggled.

Bonnie and Clyde

Criminal duo Bonnie Parker (1910–34) and Clyde Barrow (1909–34) became notorious in American newspapers for their daring armed robberies. Both originally from Texas, they teamed up in 1932 and began a series of raids on small-town banks, petrol stations, stores, and restaurants. They were finally tracked, ambushed, and gunned down by police in Louisiana in May, 1934.

Bonnie and Clyde beside their getaway car, which is riddled with bullet holes.

Both skilled and unskilled workers found it hard to get a job.

I KNOW 3 TRADES
I SPEAK 3 LANGUAGES
FOUGHT FOR 3 YEARS
HAVE 3 CHILDREN
AND NO WORK FOR
3 MONTHS
BUT I ONLY WANT
ONE JOB

THE GREAT DEPRESSION

1929
In March, US President Herbert Hoover says in his inaugural address, "In no nation are the fruits of accomplishment more secure." In October, the New York Stock Exchange crashes.

1930
The Smoot-Hawley Tariff Act raises duties, harming imports but not helping US trade.

1931
The 102-storey Empire State Building is completed in New York as the tallest building in the world. The popular song "Brother, Can You Spare a Dime?" expresses Depression feelings.

1932
Troops drive a group of protesting unemployed war veterans out of Washington. New York City Police estimate that 7,000 adults shine shoes for a living in the city.

1933
In July, share prices at last stop falling (at 15 percent of their 1929 value). End of the Prohibition period.

1934
Germany adopts a "New Plan" for trade regulated by the state.

Crowds of worried people gathered in New York streets as news of the Stock Exchange crash spread.

This British newspaper report appeared the day after the crash. It reported prices tumbling "like an avalanche."

The Wall Street Crash

Throughout the 1920s, the value of shares on the major Stock Exchange in Wall Street, New York, kept on rising. The US economy was doing extremely well. Then on 24 October, 1929, share prices suddenly fell rapidly, leading shareholders to sell their stock. This reduced prices further. The day of the Wall Street Crash came to be known as Black Thursday. Some banks lost so much money that they were forced to close, causing panic among customers. By 1932, nearly every US bank had closed.

A 1932 campaign badge for the Democratic presidential candidate, Roosevelt, who said: "I pledge you, I pledge myself, to a new deal for the American people."

A New Deal for the USA

When Roosevelt became president in 1933, he introduced a range of measures to get the United States out of its Great Depression. His New Deal of social and economic reforms aimed to restore confidence in the banks, reduce unemployment and help the poor. The programme did not solve all the problems, but it did help those facing most hardship.

I WANT YOU F.D.R.

STAY AND FINISH THE JOB!

INDEPENDENT VOTERS' COMMITTEE OF THE ARTS *and* SCIENCES *for* ROOSEVELT

FDR

Franklin Delano Roosevelt (1882–1945), known as FDR, is the only US president to be elected four times. He was in office for more than 12 years, leading his nation through World War II. He had been paralysed by poliomyelitis in 1921, but never allowed this to hold him back. Roosevelt famously said in 1933 that "the only thing we have to fear is fear itself", and he was fearless in seeing through his New Deal reforms.

The Hundred Days

Most of Roosevelt's New Deal laws were brought in between March and June 1933, a period called "the Hundred Days." First, the new president closed all the nation's banks; only financially sound ones were allowed to re-open. Then he created new agencies. The National Recovery Administration (NRA) helped businesses and workers; the Agricultural Adjustment Administration (AAA) helped farmers; and the Civilian Conservation Corps (CCC) launched a relief programme for the poor.

A NEW DEAL FOR THE USA

1933
Roosevelt's first law as president is the Emergency Banking Act. The Tennessee Valley Authority (TVA) helps control floods and generate electricity.

1934
The Securities Exchange Commission regulates the stock market.

1935
The Works Progress Administration provides jobs for more than 8 million Americans. The National Labor Relations Board helps industry and trade unions.

1936
Roosevelt wins re-election.

1937
The Farm Security Administration helps farmers buy equipment.

1938
The Fair Labor Standards Act bans child labour and sets a minimum wage.

DARRYL F. ZANUCK'S PRODUCTION OF **THE GRAPES OF WRATH** BY *John Steinbeck*

WITH **HENRY FONDA** JANE **DARWELL** JOHN **CARRADINE** CHARLEY **GRAPEWIN**

BORIS **BOWDON** RUSSELL **SIMPSON** O.Z. **WHITEHEAD** JOHN **QUALEN** EDDIE **QUILLAN** ZEFFIE **TILBURY**

20th CENTURY-FOX Encore Hit!

ASSOCIATE PRODUCER AND SCREEN PLAY BY NUNNALLY JOHNSON

DIRECTED BY **JOHN FORD**

Helping the "Forgotten Man"

Roosevelt said he wanted his government to help the "forgotten man" at the bottom of the economic heap. He was thinking of the poor and the unemployed, including those who lost their homes. In 1939 American author John Steinbeck's novel *The Grapes of Wrath* told the story of a poor farming family that was forced to leave Oklahoma and head for California in search of a better life.

Poster for the 1940 film of Steinbeck's novel. Director John Ford won an Oscar for his work.

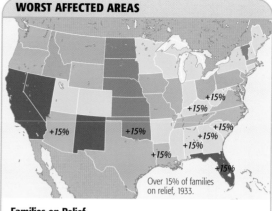

WORST AFFECTED AREAS

+15%
+15%
+15%
+15%
+15%
+15%
+15%
+15%

Over 15% of families on relief, 1933.

Families on Relief

The economic situation varied across the United States. As this map shows, in many of the southern states more than 15 per cent of families were on New Deal relief before the end of 1933. As people moved in search of work and to avoid drought and dust storms, the population in the central strip of states decreased. Many headed west.

POPULATION INCREASE AND DECREASE

■ 20% + ■ 15–20% ■ 10–15% ■ 5–10% ■ 0–5% ■ decrease

Migrant Families

Like the family in *The Grapes of Wrath*, many US farmers were badly hit by droughts and dust storms in the 1930s (see page 12). Many stuck it out as long as they could, but were eventually forced to leave their homes and try to find farming work and build new lives in other states. They packed up their possessions and set off to look for jobs pulling carrots or picking fruit or cotton.

This Oklahoma family packed up all their belongings in their car and headed for "the cotton fields of Arizona" on their way to California.

Roosevelt's "Tree Army"

The Civilian Conservation Corps (CCC) put people to work in useful projects, such as planting trees, building flood barriers and repairing forest roads. Workers were given free accommodation in camps, where they received food, medical care and a wage of a dollar a day. Altogether the CCC gave work to about 3 million men, and the "Tree Army" planted more than 3 billion new trees over 9 years.

Civilian Conservation Corps recruits planting trees in 1933. The trees replaced those destroyed by forest fires and were intended to stop erosion and dust storms caused by drought.

Rudolph Valentino played a desert chieftain opposite Agnes Ayres in The Sheik *(1921). The film was followed in 1926 by* Son of the Sheik.

Poster for the first successful talkie, which included songs such as "My Mammy."

The Silent Era

In the early 1920s, films grew in popularity as a form of mass entertainment. The growing movie studios made stars of actors such as Douglas Fairbanks Sr, Mary Pickford and Charlie Chaplin, who all worked for the United Artists studio. One of the most popular stars was the Italian-born actor Rudolph Valentino (1895–1926), who became famous for his romantic roles.

Coming of the Talkies

By 1925, several systems had been developed to add sound to films. Audiences were enthusiastic, but the studios were less convinced. Nevertheless, in 1926 Warner Bros brought out *Don Juan*, starring John Barrymore, which had a musical accompaniment recorded by the New York Philharmonic Orchestra. They followed this up the next year with *The Jazz Singer*, in which Al Jolson sang and spoke some dialogue. The new talking pictures were a huge success.

Walt Disney

Born in Chicago in 1901, Walt Disney moved to Los Angeles in 1923 to make movies. He set up a small studio and started producing cartoons with animal characters. Disney used sound and himself provided the voice for his most famous character, Mickey Mouse. In 1932 he made *Flowers and Trees* in Technicolor. Five years later, the Disney studio created the first full-length animated feature film with human characters and popular songs.

In 1932 Walt Disney won an Honorary Academy Award for Mickey Mouse and an Oscar for best short cartoon.

This famous sign was put up in Hollywood Hills in 1923.

The Hollywood Dream Factory

In the 1920s, Hollywood, a district of Los Angeles in California, became the center of the motion-picture industry. Companies that had studios there set up a system that gave them control over the entire production of their films, including the many different people involved. This led to a golden age of American films. From 1930 to 1945 Hollywood studios produced more than 7,500 movies.

Orson Welles, seated far right, directs a scene in Citizen Kane. *The film was not a financial success on release, but it received nine Oscar nominations and won Best Original Screenplay. Oscars (right) were first awarded by the Academy of Motion Picture Arts and Sciences in 1929.*

Paramount Studios in the 1930s, when the company had such star actors as Gary Cooper, Marlene Dietrich and W.C. Fields.

Big Studios

During the 1920s, films were dominated by the ever-growing big studios—Columbia, Fox, MGM, Paramount, RKO, United Artists, Universal and Warner Bros. These companies made and distributed films and owned cinemas. Their producers were tough businessmen. A studio signed up directors, writers, designers and technicians, as well as actors, so that they were on the payroll and worked only for that studio.

Greatest Film of All Time?

In 1941 one of the smallest of the major studios—RKO Radio Pictures—released a film called *Citizen Kane*. It is considered a masterpiece of cinematic technique, and in 2007 the American Film Institute made it number one in its list of all-time great US movies. The film, which is about a newspaper magnate, was directed by and starred Orson Welles (1915–85), who was given complete control over production of the film by RKO.

Genres

The studio system concentrated on genres, or specific types, of film. Westerns, gangster movies and comedies were all popular genres. Director John Ford increased the popularity of the Western with *Stagecoach* (1939). The film won two Oscars and made a star of John Wayne, who went on to make many more cowboy films. In the same year a new studio called Selznick Pictures had a sensational hit with *Gone With the Wind*, an American Civil War drama.

A famous scene from King Kong (1933), with the ape on top of the Empire State Building.

Golden Age

Popular Hollywood films provided entertainment for millions of people during the difficult period of the Depression (see pages 12–13). Actors became huge stars. As the political situation became more worrying towards the end of the 1930s, Hollywood studios made patriotic films with happy endings. This was a golden age for the studio system of movie production, and new, expensive films were heavily promoted.

Charlie Chaplin made fun of fascism in his 1940 film The Great Dictator.

THE HOLLYWOOD DREAM FACTORY

1921
Rudolph Valentino becomes a star in The Four Horsemen of the Apocalypse.

1922
Douglas Fairbanks Sr. stars in Robin Hood.

1925
Charlie Chaplin directs and stars as the Little Tramp in The Gold Rush.

1928
Disney cartoons feature Mickey Mouse for the first time.

1929
Gary Cooper stars with Walter Huston in the Western hit The Virginian.

1937
Disney issues the first full-length (83-minute) animated film, Snow White and the Seven Dwarfs.

1939
Release of Gone With the Wind, The Hunchback of Notre Dame, Stagecoach *and* The Wizard of Oz.

1940
English-born Alfred Hitchcock makes his first US film, Rebecca.

Leon Trotsky

Trotsky helped lead the 1917 revolution and was the second most powerful man in Russia, after Lenin. In the Communist government Trotsky became Commissar for Foreign Affairs and then Commissar for War. He founded the Red Army (which was named after the color of the Communist flag), recruiting workers and peasants. He appointed former officers of the imperial army to lead them. Trotsky's use of the military to overhaul the Russian railway led to opposition from trade unionists.

Russian revolutionary Leon Trotsky (1879–1940) was born Lev Davidovich Bronstein in Ukraine.

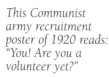

This Communist army recruitment poster of 1920 reads: "You! Are you a volunteer yet?"

Reds versus Whites

From 1918 to 1920, there was civil war in Russia. The Red Army fought against a group of anti-Communist armies (known as Whites), including Ukrainian nationalists. The Whites were politically supported by Russia's First World War allies, including Britain and France, who opposed Communism. The White armies were nowhere nearly as organized as the Reds, and by November 1920 their final group was defeated in the Crimea.

SOVIET UNION 1922–25

SOVIET UNION

MONGOLIA

CHINA

Creation of the USSR

In December 1922, the Russian government united with Communist neighbors to found the Union of Soviet Socialist Republics (USSR, or Soviet Union). There were four founding republics—Belarus, Russia, Transcaucasia (modern Azerbaijan, Armenia, and Georgia), and Ukraine. The map shows the Union's territory in its early years.

- USSR in Oct. 1922
- Gained by 1925
- Gained 30 Dec. 1922
- Gained 19 Nov. 1922
- Japanese until 1925
- Other Communist states
- Frontier of USSR in 1923

Lenin and the Bolsheviks

When the revolutionary Bolsheviks formed a new government in 1917, they promised the Russian people great changes. The new regime was led by Lenin (1870–1924, real name Vladimir Ilyich Ulyanov), who was chairman of the Council of People's Commissars. Lenin redistributed their vast country's land to the peasants, but he also saw a need for a strong central government. The Bolsheviks hoped that their revolution would lead to a spread of Communism in other Western countries.

Birth of the Soviet Union

The Bolshevik Revolution of 1917 had led to a new government in Russia, headed by Lenin. In March the following year, the Russian Communists made peace with Germany, but were forced to give up territory, including the Baltic states, Finland, Poland, and Ukraine. Lenin concentrated on the reforms promised by his party, and in 1922 Russia joined with Ukraine and two other neighboring republics to form the Soviet Union.

Lenin speaks to a crowd of supporters on May 1, 1918.

The End of Lenin's Rule

From 1922 until his death two years later, Lenin suffered strokes and poor health. This meant a period of instability as others competed for power. The undisputed winner of the contest was Stalin. The new General Secretary gained the support of other committee members to oust Trotsky, who was later expelled from the party and exiled.

Lenin's body was displayed in a glass coffin inside a wooden mausoleum beside Red Square, in Moscow. Later, the mausoleum was rebuilt in red granite (left).

Izvestia

The daily national newspaper *Izvestia* (meaning "Delivered Messages" or "News") was founded in 1917 by the Petrograd Soviet of Workers' Deputies. After the formation of the USSR, it became the official newspaper of the Soviet government, outlining policy and expressing official views. *Izvestia* survived the collapse of Communism in 1991 and is still published today.

The Izvestia building in Moscow shows the full title of the newspaper: News of Soviets of Peoples' Deputies of the USSR.

BIRTH OF THE SOVIET UNION

1918
Russia signs the Treaty of Brest-Litovsk with Germany, withdrawing from the First World War. The Bolsheviks move the Russian capital back from Petrograd (formerly St. Petersburg) to Moscow.

1919
Lenin forms the Third International, an organization of world Communist parties. Russo-Polish War (1919–20).

1920
Polish leader Jozef Pilsudski defeats the Red Army and gains western Ukraine and Belarus.

1921
Rebellion by sailors at the Kronstadt naval base is crushed by the Red Army; this leads directly to Lenin's New Economic Policy.

1922
Lenin becomes seriously ill; in March, Joseph Stalin becomes General Secretary of the Communist Party.

1923
Lenin dictates a political Testament, warning against allowing Stalin too much power.

1924
Lenin dies on January 21; Petrograd is renamed Leningrad; Turkmenistan and Uzbekistan become new Soviet republics.

Stalin's Russia

After the death of Lenin and a victorious power struggle over Trotsky and others, Joseph Stalin gained total power. From 1929 he ruled unopposed as dictator of the Soviet Union. Stalin lived up to his adopted name of "man of steel," murdering opponents and sending millions to labor camps. His bold plans for industrialization were largely successful, but his hard-line policies for increasing agricultural output were disastrous, costing millions of lives.

This Soviet statue of 1935 represents successful industry and agriculture.

Young Stalin met with other revolutionaries and learned political skills, such as knowing which colleagues to trust.

Rise to Supreme Power

Stalin was born in Georgia, the son of a shoemaker and a washerwoman. He trained to be a priest before joining a secret Marxist group and, later, the Bolsheviks. He played an important part in the revolution of 1917, which was led by Lenin and Trotsky; after gaining power Stalin claimed to have been Lenin's co-leader. After becoming General Secretary of the Communist Party in 1922, Stalin set about gaining supreme power over the Soviet Union.

Peasants and Workers

Stalin planned to get farmers to produce enough grain to feed workers in the cities, so that industry could expand. Peasants were forced to give up ownership of their plots of land and work with others on large collective farms, which belonged to the state. Fewer unskilled farm laborers were needed, so many were sent to work in the growing factories. Those peasants who resisted were sent to labor camps or killed.

Women worked on collective farms, as well as in factories.

Many new factories were built following the first Five Year Plan. Millions of workers moved to the growing cities to push through increased production.

Coalminer Alexei Stakhanov was said by the Soviet leadership to have cut 15 times more coal than other workers in a single shift, and was held up as a model for others to follow.

End of the Kulaks

The kulaks were a class of wealthy landowning peasants who could afford to hire labour and lease portions of their land. They had been important people before the revolution, and they opposed Stalin's policy of collectivization (creating collective farms). The kulaks' land and property were taken by force, and they joined many of their former laborers in the Soviet gulags (labour camps).

Prisoners were forced to work hard in freezing conditions in the gulags of Siberia. Conditions were harsh, food was poor, and many died in the camps.

Andrey Vishinsky was the chief prosecutor in Stalin's purge trials of the 1930s. He was greatly feared by those accused of treason.

Regime of Terror

In 1934, Stalin began increasing his fight against anyone who opposed him. He ruthlessly got rid of the old Bolsheviks who had supported and been close to Lenin. Then he set about eliminating all his political opponents and those who threatened his power, including top generals and thousands of other army officers. Many were put on trial, but they were not given a fair hearing. They were simply forced to "confess," and were then executed.

Plans for Industry

In 1928, Stalin launched his first Five Year Plan for economic development. The aim was to increase coal and steel production, as well as the production of machinery and farm equipment. This meant producing fewer household goods and clothing. In order to achieve the Plan, private businesses were taken over by the state, which set production targets. Further Five Year Plans created more factories, as industrial production increased.

COLLECTIVIZATION 1923–39

Agricultural Reform

By 1933 more than three-quarters of the Soviet Union's independent farms had been turned into collectives and were controlled by the state (see map). But resistance to this had terrible consequences. There was famine in the south and east, which killed up to 4 million people in the Ukraine republic alone. Peasants who resisted collectivization were sent to labor camps all over the country.

- 2–10% of all farms collectivized by 1928
- 25–50% of all farms collectivized by 1933
- 50–70% of all farms collectivized by 1933
- 70-85% of all farms collectivized by 1933

STALIN'S RUSSIA

1913
Iosif Dzhugashvili changes his name to Stalin, meaning "man of steel."

1924
Lenin's Testament (warning of Stalin) is read by the Central Committee, but Stalin survives as General Secretary.

1925
Stalin publicly attacks Trotsky for being unfaithful to the principles of Lenin.

1932
People's Commissariats (for the heavy, light and timber industries) carry on the Five Year Plan.

1932–33
Terrible famine in which many millions die.

1934
Communist leader Sergey Kirov is murdered, marking the beginning of Stalin's Great Purge.

1936
Grigori Zinoviev is retried in a show trial for the murder of Kirov and executed.

1937–38
Many thousands of Russian Orthodox priests are persecuted, and remaining churches close.

1938
Trotsky founds the Fourth International in opposition to Stalin (and two years later is murdered in Mexico by a Soviet agent).

1939
At the 18th Party Congress, in March, Stalin announces the end of the Great Purge.

Fascism in Italy

Fascist Italian flag flying from a fasces.

Fascism is an authoritarian, nationalistic political movement and system of government. It takes its name from the fasces, a bundle of rods that represented the authority of ancient Rome. The movement was first introduced in Italy by Mussolini, who used the chaos and depression of the 1920s to gain support from landowners and industrialists, as well as extremists who cared little for equality and individual liberty.

Mussolini and his Blackshirts, photographed in 1922. The armed squads became more violent as they gained power.

Painting showing the bombing of Ethiopia by the Italian air force.

Colonial Empire

Mussolini was determined to increase Italy's influence as a major power. In 1935–36 Italian forces invaded Emperor Haile Selassie's Abyssinia (modern Ethiopia), despite opposition from the League of Nations. Other European countries opposed Italy's colonial policies, but they received backing from Germany. In 1939, Italy conquered Albania, which remained part of the Italian Empire until the Germans took over four years later.

The Leader

In 1922, large numbers of Blackshirts marched on Rome. The Italian king, Victor Emmanuel III, feared a civil war and felt forced to appoint Mussolini prime minister. Three years later, Mussolini declared a dictatorship, with himself at the head. He was called "Il Duce" (the Leader). Other political parties were banned, and the Fascist government took control of the police, industry, and the press.

Two Fascist leaders: Il Duce (Mussolini) and Der Führer (Hitler).

Mussolini's Rise to Power

Benito Mussolini (1883–1945) started off believing in socialism, and at the age of 29 edited the left-wing Italian Socialist Party's newspaper. He served in the Italian army in the First World War, before founding the Italian Fascist Party, which combined socialist and extreme right-wing ideas. The Fascists were supported by black-shirted armed squads, who at first terrorized Communists and went on to target all opponents of Mussolini and fascism.

Rome–Berlin Axis

The Italian dictator was supported in his ambitions by the dictator of Germany, Adolf Hitler. In 1936, they both sent troops to support the Spanish Fascist dictator, Francisco Franco. Hitler and Mussolini announced a Rome–Berlin Axis (or center of power), around which they believed other European states would gather. The Axis was further strengthened by the addition of Japan in the Tripartite Pact of 1940.

Mussolini had an office in the prestigious Palazzo Venezia in central Rome.

Desperate Downfall

In 1943, after Allied troops landed in Sicily, the Fascist Grand Council dismissed Mussolini and restored the king to power. Mussolini was imprisoned and then rescued by German soldiers. The former dictator became a German puppet ruler of the so-called Italian Social Republic in the north of the country. As World War II neared its end, Mussolini was captured by Italian anti-Fascist partisans and executed.

Opponents of the Fascist regime were terrorized, tortured, and killed.

ITALIAN EMPIRE, 1939

ITALY
ALBANIA
LIBYA
ERITREA
ABYSSINIA
SOMALILAND

Italian Empire, 1939

Mussolini's Colonies

Italy had controlled Libya since 1912 and the small Dodecanese islands off Turkey since 1923. Mussolini's Fascist regime took Albania and expanded the region known as Italian East Africa. Italian troops added Abyssinia (Ethiopia) by invading without warning from areas already controlled by Italy—Somaliland (Somalia) and Eritrea.

Economic Aims

Mussolini's Fascists introduced programmes to improve the economy by helping agriculture and creating employment. The "Battle for grain" program used existing and new farmland for growing the wheat that was needed to make Italy self-sufficient. The "Battle for land" reclaimed large areas of marshland, which were then used for farming. As the government took control of the economy, many Italian people welcomed its strong leadership and reforms.

A Fascist demonstration in Milan's Galleria arcade in 1934. Mussolini was presented by the Fascist Party as a great leader who could bring enormous success to Italy.

FASCISM IN ITALY

1919
Mussolini founds the Fascist Combat Group.

1921
The Blackshirts join the Fascist Party as a national militia.

1926
Secret police and political courts are established.

1929
Lateran Treaties between Mussolini's government and Pope Pius XI.

1936
The Rome–Berlin Axis is proclaimed.

1937
Italy joins Germany and Japan in an alliance against the Soviet Union.

1939
Italy and Germany make a formal alliance known as the Pact of Steel.

1940
Italy declares war on Britain and France and enters World War II.

1941
British forces help the Ethiopians drive Italians out of their country.

1943
In September, Italy surrenders to the Allies.

1945
Mussolini is shot; his body is hung upside down for display in Milan.

Reshaping the Middle East

The collapse of the Ottoman Empire in the early 20th century led to the foundation of the new republic of Turkey. The League of Nations divided other parts of the former empire into so-called mandated territories, administered by Britain and France. This approach caused conflict with Arab nationalists, and Jewish immigration heightened the tension in Palestine. Unsolved problems in the Middle East left a lasting legacy of conflict.

The Balfour Declaration (see below) was made in a letter from the British foreign secretary, Arthur James Balfour, to Lord Rothschild.

BRITISH MANDATES

SYRIA

Palestine

Transjordan

BRITISH MANDATE OF PALESTINE

ARABIA

Palestine and Transjordan

The Balfour Declaration of 1917 stated British support for the establishment in Palestine of a national home for the Jewish people. Three years later, the UK was given a mandate to govern the whole region of Palestine (see map). In 1922, Palestine was limited to the area west of the River Jordan, and the area to the east became Transjordan.

In 1919, the Zionist politician Chaim Weizmann (left, wearing Arab clothing as a sign of friendship) signed an agreement of Jewish-Arab cooperation with Emir Faisal (later king of Iraq).

End of the Ottoman Empire

Defeat in the First World War meant that the Ottomans lost all their territory outside Asia Minor. By the end of the war Britain and France occupied much of the Middle East region of the former empire. This led to the League of Nations going on to create the states of Iraq, Palestine and Transjordan (later Jordan) as mandated territories administered by Britain, while Lebanon and Syria came under French administration.

New Dynasty in Persia

The kingdom of Persia, which had been ruled by shahs of the Qajar dynasty since 1794, remained neutral during the First World War. In 1921 the Qajar government was overthrown and a cavalry officer named Reza Khan came to power. From 1925 he reigned as the Shah of Persia, and 10 years later the country changed its name to Iran (or "land of the Aryans").

The Golestan Palace in the Persian capital of Tehran once belonged to a group of royal Qajar buildings.

Kemal Atatürk (1881–1938), founder of modern Turkey.

Birth of Modern Turkey

The people of the region that remained of the former Ottoman Empire resented harsh treatment by the Greeks and their allies. In 1922, nationalist forces drove the Greeks from the region and abolished the office of sultan formerly held by the Ottoman rulers. They announced the new republic of Turkey and elected the nationalist hero Mustafa Kemal as president, naming him Atatürk–"Father of the Turks."

Desert Kingdom

The deserts of the Arabian peninsula had been controlled by tribal leaders and the Ottomans. From 1902, the Saud family gained control over more and more territory, but the British administered the region as a protectorate from 1915. Ibn Saud gained the holy cities of Mecca and Medina in 1925, and set about bringing the desert provinces together. By 1932, he was able to proclaim the lands under his control as the Kingdom of Saudi Arabia.

Oil was discovered in Saudi Arabia in 1936, changing the new kingdom's fortunes. The picture shows the first Saudi well gushing oil.

Colonial and Arab Disputes

King Faisal I of Iraq (ruled 1921–33) was a leader of Arab nationalism. The British government supported him as an influential statesman who could govern an independent Iraq after the British mandate ended in 1932. Since Iraq shared a long border with Saudi Arabia, British leaders attempted to bring about a settlement of old disputes between the two kingdoms. Agreements were reached, but future troubles were to prove that these were often short-lived.

RISING TENSION

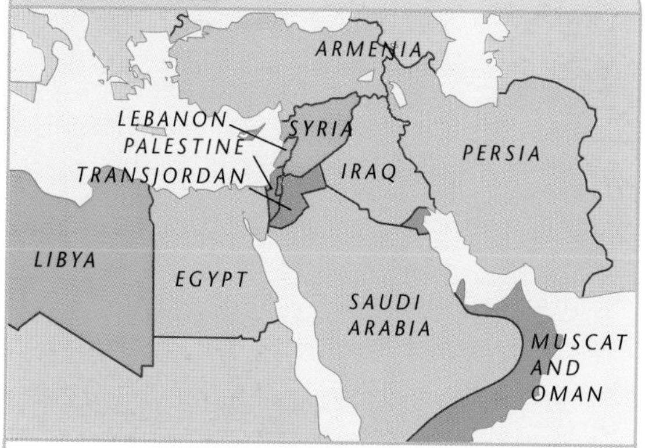

Map showing: ARMENIA, LEBANON, PALESTINE, TRANSJORDAN, SYRIA, IRAQ, PERSIA, LIBYA, EGYPT, SAUDI ARABIA, MUSCAT AND OMAN

By 1939, many of the countries of the Middle East region had officially gained independence, but some of the region was still administered by colonial powers (see map). Many Arab people were pressing for independence. They included the Palestinian Arabs, who protested about the increasing numbers of Jewish immigrants from Nazi Germany during the 1930s.

MANDATORY POWERS AND INDEPENDENT COUNTRIES, 1939

Italy   Britain   France   Independent country

In 1930, Faisal I of Iraq met Ibn Saud of Saudi Arabia aboard a British warship in the Gulf. The meeting, hosted by the British High Commissioner to Iraq and an RAF air marshal, ended in both sides recognizing the other's territory.

Britain's Imperial Sunset

Though Britain emerged from the First World War victorious, its human casualties, financial costs, and devastation left the country facing huge problems at home. Abroad, many of the United Kingdom's colonies were calling for independence, threatening the authority of the formerly all-powerful British Empire. Ireland became independent, along with other founder members of the Commonwealth of Nations, and Britain lost authority in India.

Londoners celebrate the end of the Great War.

The Irish nationalist Michael Collins (1890–1922) became prime minister of the Irish Free State. He was killed by Republicans who opposed the Anglo-Irish Treaty.

After transport workers joined the General Strike, the government ordered armed escorts for important food convoys.

Poster for the "Abundance of Africa," part of the British Empire Exhibition of 1924–25.

Independence for Ireland

In 1921, after years of fighting, Ireland was split into the British dominion of the Irish Free State and the Ulster counties of Northern Ireland, which remained part of the United Kingdom. The Irish Free State gradually cut its ties with the UK, and by 1937 was ready to gain full independence as Eire.

British Empire Exhibition

The aim of this exhibition, held at Wembley in 1924–25, was to strengthen trade with the colonies. At the opening ceremony, King George V sent a telegram that traveled right round the world in just over a minute. The three main buildings, linked by a "never-stop" railway, were devoted to industry, engineering and the arts. The exhibition attracted 27 million visitors.

General Strike

Britain faced severe economic problems after the War. The coal industry was hard hit, and when mine-owners cut wages and called for longer hours in 1926, the Trades Union Congress backed a General Strike. This lasted only nine days before the trade unionists accepted defeat, but the miners stayed out for another six months. Conservative Chancellor of the Exchequer Winston Churchill vigorously opposed the strike, which ended in failure for the workers.

BRITISH EMPIRE, 1921

Rule Britannia

In 1921, the British Empire covered more than a quarter of the globe (see map). But there was a move towards independence in the self-governing colonies, recognized by an Imperial Conference declaration in 1926. Five years later, Australia, Canada, the Irish Free State, New Zealand, Newfoundland, and South Africa became independent within the new Commonwealth of Nations.

◼ British Empire in 1921

India

During the 1920s, Mohandas Gandhi and the Indian National Congress party pushed forward a programme of non-violent opposition to British rule. They encouraged civil disobedience, non-cooperation and a boycott of British goods. By 1935, Indians had more representation in provincial lawmaking and government, but the British viceroy still held overall power. Nevertheless, the independence movement was gathering pace, as the British Empire faced the loss of its "jewel in the crown."

Mohandas Gandhi (1869–1948), known as Mahatma ("great soul"), believed in self-reliance and simplicity. A British-educated lawyer, Gandhi was imprisoned several times in India.

Constitutional Crisis

Crisis struck the British establishment after Edward VILI succeeded his father, King George V, who died in 1936. Before his coronation, Edward let it be known that he wanted to marry an American divorcee, Mrs Wallis Simpson. Prime Minister Stanley Baldwin, the Archbishop of Canterbury and many other important people objected, and Edward gave up the throne. Following the abdication, his brother became George VI.

In the 1930s, British banks issued brass money boxes like this one to encourage saving. Only the bank could open the box.

BRITAIN'S IMPERIAL SUNSET

1919
Republicans declare Ireland independent, leading to fighting between Irish rebels (the Irish Republican Army or IRA) and British forces.

1921
Anglo-Irish Treaty gives British dominion status to a new Irish Free State.

1922–23
Civil war in Ireland.

1924
Britain has its first Labour administration, relying on Liberal support.

1927
The Trade Disputes Act (repealed in 1946) makes general strikes illegal.

1930
Gandhi leads the Salt March to the sea, protesting against British taxes on salt manufacture.

1931
The Statute of Westminster establishes the Commonwealth of Nations.

1937
The Muslim League grows in popularity and power in India.

The former Edward VILI married Wallis Simpson in France in 1937. They became the Duke and Duchess of Windsor.

China in Turmoil

The Communist revolutionary leader, Mao Zeroing (1893–1976).

In the early 1920s, much of the republic of China was ruled by warlords (regional military leaders), but soon there were great changes. The Nationalists exercised their power over the warlords, and the Communists organized themselves into a strong force. Civil war broke out between the two political powers, and the Nationalists and Communists were only brought together by a common enemy—Japan.

Chinese peasants were so poor that they could afford little farming equipment.

Mao Zeroing

Mao was born into a farming family in southern China. From the age of 7, he worked in his father's fields. He was 18 when rebels overthrew the imperial government and made China a republic. In 1921, Mao was one of the 12 founding members of the Chinese Communist Party in Shanghai. The young Communists wanted to unite their country by joining up with the Kuomintang (Nationalist Party).

Civil War

In 1927 war broke out between Chiang Kai-shek's Nationalists, based at their capital in Nanjing, and Mao's Communists, based in Shanghai. Chiang led a number of campaigns that were designed to wipe out his Communist rivals, including a massacre of Shanghai workers. Mao led hundreds of peasants to the mountains of Jiangxi province, in southeastern China. They formed the beginnings of the People's Liberation (or Red) Army.

Just like the Communists, Nationalist soldiers had to survive tough conditions and had a poor diet.

Postage stamp showing a portrait of Chiang Kai-shek.

ROUTE OF THE LONG MARCH

Shaanxi
• BEIJING
Huang He
• YAN'AN
• TSINING
C H I N A
• CHENGDU   SHANGHAI •
Jangtsekiang
Jiangxi
• JUICHIN
TAIPEI •
• GUANGZHOU

Chiang Kai-shek

Chiang Kai-shek (1887–1975), also known as Jiang Jieshi, was the son of a village merchant. As a young man he attended the Chinese Imperial Military Academy, and in 1923 ran his own military academy. Three years later, he was commander-in-chief of the National Revolutionary Army. Chiang led the successful Northern Expedition, a military campaign against powerful warlords in northern China.

From Jiangxi to Shaanxi

Mao's Long March (see page 29) began when about 100,000 Communists left their base, broke through Nationalist lines and headed west. Their route then turned north (see map). Altogether the Communist troops crossed 18 mountain ranges and 24 rivers, covering about 6,000 miles (9,700 km) in a year and 5 days.

—— Route of Mao's Long March

This painting shows some of the women who made the Long March. They return enemy fire as they start to cross one of the many rivers along the way.

Japanese Invasion

In 1931, the Japanese invaded and occupied the huge northeastern province of Manchuria. Six years later Japanese forces moved further inland, causing Chinese Communists and Nationalists to unite against the invaders. Japan's army was better equipped than its opponents and soon captured Shanghai. As Nanjing fell, many thousands of men, women and children were massacred. The Sino-Japanese War was to carry on until 1945.

Cartoon illustrating the Japanese aggressive attitude towards its much bigger neighbor.

This calendar for year 23 of the Chinese Republic (1933), based on the lunar cycle, gives guidance on favorable days.

The Long March

By 1934, the Communists had suffered heavy losses in the civil war, and Mao Zedong's group was close to collapse. Mao's Communist army, together with 35 women, decided to move north. They were bombarded by the Nationalist air force and ground troops, and about half were killed in the first three months of the Long March. They were joined by other small Communist groups along the way, but only about 8,000 marchers completed the hazardous journey, which ended in Shaanxi province. The Long March strengthened Mao's leadership of the Communist Party and inspired many young Chinese to join him.

CHINA IN TURMOIL

1918
Mao Zeroing works as a library assistant at Beijing University and learns about Communism.

1919
Beijing students demonstrate against the Versailles Peace Conference (especially against Japan keeping previous German-held territory).

1923
Sun Yat-sen, head of the Nationalist Party, reorganizes the Party and Army with help from the Soviet Union.

1924
Sun Yat-sen establishes a short-lived United Front of Communists and Nationalists.

1925
Police clashes with students lead to a general strike in Shanghai. Death of Sun Yat-sen.

1935
The Chinese Communist Party confirms Mao Zeroing in the new post of chairman.

1936
Chiang Kai-shek is imprisoned by one of his own generals for 13 days.

1937
Beginning of the Sino–Japanese War, causing a second (and more successful) United Front of Chinese forces; the Soviet Union and China sign a non-aggression pact.

1938
The Japanese take Guangzhou (Canton).

Civil War in Spain

After Spain became a republic in 1931, there was a widening gap between the political left and right wings. The Communists on the left sympathized with Republican aims, while the Fascists of the extreme right and the Catholic Church supported the Nationalists. Liberal ideals came up against authoritarian power, and the Civil War of 1936–39 tore the country apart. By the time the Nationalist commander General Franco was victorious, about 700,000 people had died in the struggle.

Many civilians took up arms in the war, using guerrilla tactics.

Poster of the Iberian Anarchist Federation (founded in 1927), which joined the fight against the Nationalists.

New Republic

King Alfonso XIII (1886–1941) ruled Spain during a period of dictatorship and social unrest. When Republican leaders won parliamentary elections in 1931, Alfonso was forced to leave the country. The government introduced a democratic constitution for the new republic, separating the state from the Church and giving more rights and freedom to the people, especially women. There was a new flag and a new anthem.

Republicans Versus Nationalists

In 1936 a military revolt against the Republican government was led by General Franco. The rebel Nationalists were supported by the Fascist party, Falange, which wanted to overthrow the democratic system. Republican loyalists resisted the takeover, leading to the violent conflict of civil war. In this battle of ideologies, Nazi Germany and Fascist Italy helped Franco's forces, while the Communist Soviet Union supported the Republicans. The US, UK, and France remained neutral.

General Francisco Franco (1892–1975), known as El Caudillo (the Leader).

General Franco

The son of a naval officer, Francisco Franco attended an infantry academy and became the youngest captain in the Spanish army in 1915. He commanded units in Morocco, where he put down rebellion against Spanish rule. Franco was promoted to brigadier general and became chief of general staff. In 1936 he led Spanish troops from Morocco to overthrow the Republican government.

SPAIN, 1936–39

LA CORUÑA
OVIEDO • X
X • GUERNICA
FRANCE
BASQUE TERRITORIES
• VALLADOLID
BARCELONA •
PORTUGAL
X • GUADALAJARA   X • GANDESA
BRUNETE • X X • MADRID
X • TERUEL
VALENCIA •
• MÉRIDA
• SEVILLE
• GRANADA
• Ceuta
SPANISH-MOROCCO

Nationalist Gains

When war broke out, the Republicans controlled most of the east and north of the country. The map (left) shows how the Spanish Nationalists changed the situation and gained territory over the next 3 years. Important battles were fought in the heart of Spain, around the capital Madrid, as loyalists and rebels struggled for control.

NATIONALIST TERRITORIAL GAINS BY:

| ▮ July 21, 1936 | ▮ Dec 31, 1937 | February, 1939 | ▮ Republican March 1939 | X Important battles |

SPANISH CIVIL WAR

1931
Niceto Alcalá Zamora (1877–1949) is elected president of the Second Republic (the First Spanish Republic was 1873–74).

1932
An autonomous government is established in Catalonia.

1933
The extreme Nationalist political group Falange ("phalanx") is founded.

1934
Franco is promoted to major general (and a year later is appointed chief of the Spanish army's general staff).

1936
Salvador Dalí, one of the few artists to support the Nationalists, takes part in the London International Surrealist Exhibition.

1937
The Vatican recognizes Franco's Nationalist regime.

1938
International Brigades (about 20,000 non-Spanish volunteers, mainly Communists) fight for the Republicans, but the Soviet Union ends large-scale aid.

1939
Franco's dictatorship starts (lasts until 1975).

Pablo Picasso's painting Guernica shows the horrors of the Civil War. In 1937 the historic Basque town of Guernica was virtually destroyed by German bombers supporting the Nationalists.

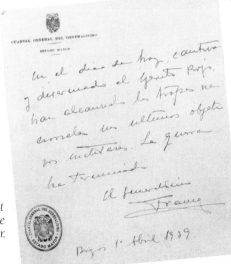

Franco's signed document declaring victory and the end of the war.

Nationalist Dictatorship

General Franco's forces took Barcelona in January 1939 and Madrid, one of the last Republican strongholds, two months later. The remaining Republican forces surrendered on April 1, leaving the Nationalists triumphant. Franco became head of state and the Falange was the only legal party in the new dictatorship. When the Second World War broke out later in the year, Spain remained neutral, although Franco's sympathies lay with Hitler's Germany.

Spanish poet and dramatist Federico Garcia Lorca (1898–1936) was shot and killed by Nationalists at the start of the Civil War.

Writers and Artists

Most Spanish writers and artists identified with the more liberal aims of the Republicans, and the government ran special missions to help young artists escape to the countryside. Sympathizers included the painters Pablo Picasso and Joan Miró (both living in France), filmmaker Luis Buñuel and writer Garcia Lorca. Foreign Republican supporters included the American novelist Ernest Hemingway and English writer George Orwell, who described his experiences in his personal account of the war, *Homage to Catalonia*.

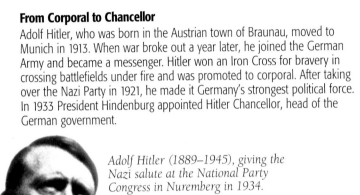

The Nazis were proud of their murderous "Night of the Long Knives."

Hitler's Rise to Power

I n the early 1920s, raging inflation ruined its currency. Then, when Germany failed to pay reparations for the Great War, France occupied the Ruhr region. The German economy collapsed and in 1933 the National Socialist German Workers' (or Nazi) Party used this desperate situation to gain power. The party's leader was Adolf Hitler, a former army corporal who rose to become the brutal dictator of Nazi Germany.

The Hakenkreuz ("hooked cross" or swastika) was an ancient symbol adopted by the Nazis.

From Corporal to Chancellor

Adolf Hitler, who was born in the Austrian town of Braunau, moved to Munich in 1913. When war broke out a year later, he joined the German Army and became a messenger. Hitler won an Iron Cross for bravery in crossing battlefields under fire and was promoted to corporal. After taking over the Nazi Party in 1921, he made it Germany's strongest political force. In 1933 President Hindenburg appointed Hitler Chancellor, head of the German government.

Adolf Hitler (1889–1945), giving the Nazi salute at the National Party Congress in Nuremberg in 1934.

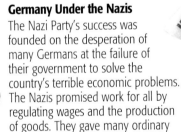

Germany Under the Nazis

The Nazi Party's success was founded on the desperation of many Germans at the failure of their government to solve the country's terrible economic problems. The Nazis promised work for all by regulating wages and the production of goods. They gave many ordinary Germans a sense of unity and power, but at the same time smothered all opposition.

The Nazis manipulated public opinion by taking over the media and using extreme propaganda.

Night of the Long Knives

On 30 June 1934, the SS (Schutzstaffel, "protective unit") murdered many of Hitler's political opponents. Most of the victims belonged to the SA (Sturmabteilung, "assault division") Brownshirts, founded by Hitler himself 13 years earlier. Hitler announced that 77 individuals had been executed for conspiracy, including SA leader Ernst Röhm. The SS arrested and murdered many more, such as former chancellor, Kurt von Schleicher.

Hitler Youth

German boys were supposed to join the Hitler Youth at age 13. They were trained in sport, camping and other activities, and strict discipline was enforced. Girls joined the League of German Maidens, where they learned gymnastics and were prepared for motherhood. By 1938, nearly 8 million young people had joined, but there were disagreements with schools that tried to keep up a more liberal tradition.

Children joined the German Young People's organization at age 10, before moving on to the older boys' or girls' group.

Poster for the 1936 Olympic Games.

Racism and Persecution

Hitler and the Nazis used the Gestapo and SS to get rid of the groups they considered "non-Aryan," so that they could promote the idea of the German nation's "racial purity." The Gestapo had unlimited powers to hound and arrest Jews, trade unionists, homosexuals, gypsies, disabled people, and left-wing intellectuals. Discrimination against these groups quickly turned into persecution, and in 1935 rights were taken away from all German Jews. Many persecuted people left Germany.

Marlene Dietrich (1901–92) was one of the most famous people to leave Germany. She went to Hollywood to star in many films.

Jews were forced to wear a yellow star on their clothes.

Berlin Olympics

For the Nazis, the 1936 Olympics made an opportunity to show the world that German athletes represented a superior race. "Non-Aryans" were kept out of the German team. Yet the Nazis tried to show their country to foreigners as a tolerant, peaceful place. Though Germany won most gold medals—33 to the USA's 24—the most successful athlete was a black American named Jesse Owens, who won four golds. Hitler avoided those medal presentation.

German Resistance

Opposition to Hitler and the Nazi Party was treason according to laws introduced in 1933. Nevertheless, some Communists, trade unionists and others distributed anti-Nazi leaflets. The Catholic Church opposed Hitler's program to kill physically and mentally disabled people, and clergymen and others helped and protected Jews.

Brother and sister Hans and Sophie Scholl (shown in the center of the poster, left), joined with university students and professors in Munich to form a resistance group known as the White Rose. They were both captured and killed during the war.

In 1937, this anti-Nazi leaflet, headed "The final appeal," was sent secretly to France concealed inside a seed packet.

HITLER'S RISE TO POWER

1921
Hitler takes over the National Socialist German Workers' Party (founded two years earlier); foundation of the SA Brownshirts.

1923
Hitler's "beer-hall putsch" fails in Munich and he is sentenced to five years in prison (serving only nine months), where he writes Mein Kampf ("My Struggle").

1925
Formation of the SS as Hitler's personal bodyguard.

1932
Hitler challenges Paul von Hindenburg for the presidency, but fails.

1933
Fire destroys the Reichstag (parliament) building in Berlin. Hermann Göring forms the Gestapo (Geheime Staatspolizei, secret state police).

1934
Death of Hindenburg and end of the Weimar Republic; Hitler announces the Third Reich (or Empire, following the first Holy Roman Empire and the second German Empire of 1871–1918).

1936
Germany rearms and occupies the Rhineland.

1937
Hitler outlines secret plans to military leaders for the conquest of Austria and Czechoslovakia.

Germany Expands

Once he had total power, Hitler put his expansionist plans into action. In 1936 his forces occupied the Rhineland region, which had been demilitarized after the First World War. German troops met with no effective opposition from France or the League of Nations. Next on Hitler's list was Austria, which he invaded in March 1938 and proclaimed Anschluss (a forced "union" with Austria). A majority of Austrians welcomed becoming part of Großdeutschland ("Greater Germany").

The League of Nations headquarters in Geneva, Switzerland.

An Ailing Peacekeeper

The League of Nations had no armed forces and had already shown itself to be powerless in the face of international aggression. Germany and Japan had left the League in 1933, and Italy joined them in 1937, to form an alliance against the Soviet Union. The Munich Agreement, signed by League members Britain and France, showed the organization's weakness against aggression.

World War II Breaks Out

As Hitler expanded his Third Reich, Britain and France became increasingly alarmed. After Austria fell to Germany, the British and French premiers tried to appease Hitler in order to avoid war. Six months later, Hitler broke that agreement and took Czechoslovakia. In September 1939, the Germans continued their aggressive expansion by invading Poland. This time Britain and France felt they had to defend their ally and respond. They declared war on Germany.

Hitler salutes his troops at a 1934 parade in Nuremberg.

Neville Chamberlain waves a copy of the Munich Agreement, which he said would mean "peace in our time."

Munich Agreement

In September 1938, British prime minister Neville Chamberlain met Hitler at Berchtesgaden, Bad Godesberg and finally Munich. They were joined in Munich by the Italian leader Benito Mussolini and French premier Edouard Daladier. Hitler wanted to take over the German-speaking region of Czechoslovakia called Sudetenland and give other Czechs the right to join the Third Reich. Britain and France wanted peace, and the agreement on Sudetenland was signed.

Night of Broken Glass

On November 7, 1938, a Jewish student from Poland shot a German diplomat in Paris. The German Propaganda Minister Joseph Goebbels used this as an excuse to encourage stormtroopers to take revenge on the Jewish communities of Germany and Austria. Two days later, Nazis smashed the windows of Jewish businesses and burned down synagogues. Thousands of Jews were terrorized throughout a night of persecution called Kristallnacht ("Crystal night").

Passers-by survey the damage of Kristallnacht in Nuremberg.

Invasion of Poland

Despite an existing non-aggression pact, Hitler invaded Poland in 1939. Britain issued an ultimatum, and when Hitler ignored it, the British and French declared war on Germany. The Second World War in Europe had begun, and British prime minister Neville Chamberlain spoke of "evil things that we shall be fighting against, brute force, bad faith, injustice, oppression, and persecution." The German form of war, later called Blitzkrieg ("lightning war"), using fast mobile ground forces with air support, overwhelmed the Polish armies.

1938

In February, Hitler demands that Austrian chancellor Kurt von Schuschnigg admit Nazis into his cabinet; Schuschnigg resigns. In March, the forced union with Austria (Anschluss) takes place. In October, Sudetenland becomes part of the Third Reich.

1939

Germany invades Czechoslovakia in March, and makes most of the country a German protectorate. In August, the Soviet Union signs a non-aggression pact with Germany. On September 1st, Hitler attacks Poland. On September 3rd, Britain, France, Australia, and New Zealand declare war on Germany. The Soviet Union joins the attack on Poland on September 17. German air raids on Britain begin in October. In December, the League of Nations expels the Soviet Union for its attack on Finland.

Polish troops in W... resisted the Ger... until the e... September... photograph below s... Polish generals sign... ceasefire agreemen... surrendering to Ge... General Joh... Blasko...

The Growing Third Reich

By September 1939, Germany had already taken over Austria and Czechoslovakia. Its attack on Poland from the west was joined by a Russian invasion from the east. This was the situation at the start of World War II (see map, right). The defeated Polish government fled first to Romania and then to Britain.

...ft: Jewish children in the Warsaw ghetto in ...41. Polish Jews in large cities were rounded ... and locked in enclosed areas. In Warsaw ...re were more than 400,000 people living ... the ghetto. In 1943, they organized the ...st armed uprising against the Nazis.

GERMANY, SEPTEMBER 1939

- ■ Allies
- ■ Germany (including Czechoslovakia)
- ■ Soviet Union
- ■ Poland – German aggression
- ■ Poland – Soviet aggression

GREAT BRITAIN

SOVIET UNION

POLAND

GERMANY

FRANCE

HITLER'S WAR TO THE WEST AND EAST

1940
In April, Germany invades Denmark and Norway; in May, Germany invades the Netherlands and France; in June, Italy declares war on Britain and France; 12 days later, France signs an armistice with Germany. In October, German U-boats sink 32 British ships in the Atlantic in a week.

1941
In April, Germany invades Greece and Yugoslavia, and in June invades the Soviet Union. German troops blockade Leningrad in September. In December, Hitler declares war on the United States.

1942
In August, Hitler orders his army to capture Stalingrad. October 23 sees the start of the Battle of El Alamein, in Egypt, which the British win.

1943
41 German U-boats are destroyed in the Atlantic in May. In September, Italy surrenders to the Allies.

1944
Allies land troops at Anzio, Italy, in January. June 6th is D-Day, the Allied invasion of German-occupied Normandy.

Hitler's War to the West and East

The Second World War began as a European conflict between the Allies (Britain and France) and Nazi Germany (in a non-aggression alliance with the Soviet Union). The Germans were joined by Italy and gained France, and by 1942 much of mainland Europe was under their control. But the situation changed dramatically when Hitler turned on Stalin. This left the Axis Powers (Germany and its partners) facing hostility to the west and the east in Europe, while the Allies were also making progress in North Africa.

Winston Churchill (1874–1965), prime minister of Britain during World War II.

A German Messerschmitt fighter is chased by an RAF Spitfire over the south coast of England during the Battle of Britain.

The German pocket battleship Admiral Graf Spee *sank in the Atlantic, off Uruguay, in December 1939.*

Battle of the Atlantic

The struggle for control of the Atlantic supply routes from America went on from 1940 to 1944. German U-boats were the main threat to British merchant ships. One of the most important battles took place in May 1941, when British ships and aircraft eventually sank the Bismarck, a powerful German battleship that was intended to raid the sea lanes.

General Patton discussing strategy after US troops landed in Sicily in 1943.

Nazi-Soviet Pact

In August 1939, foreign ministers Vyacheslav Molotov of the Soviet Union and Joachim von Ribbentrop of Germany signed a military agreement in Moscow. Each side promised not to attack the other, to remain neutral if the other was attacked, and not to join any alliance against the other. They also agreed how to divide Poland after its capture. The pact gave Hitler the confidence to attack in September 1939.

Von Ribbentrop stands behind Molotov, as he signs the Nazi-Soviet Pact. Stalin (right), who was pleased with the pact's terms, looks on.

WAR IN EUROPE, 1942–44

Fall of Berlin May 1945

Battle of Stalingrad 1942–43

D-DAY June 6, 1944

BERLIN

• STALINGRAD

Invasion of south of France August 1944

Invasion of Italy Sept. 1943

Battle of El-Alamein Nov. 1942

Invasion of Sicily July 1943

Operation Torch invasion of NW Africa Nov. 1942

• EL-ALAMEIN

Advances and Gains

When Hitler broke with Stalin and invaded Russia, he committed Germany to war on two fronts. The map shows how the territory controlled by the Axis Powers expanded in the first three years of the war. But Germany itself was squeezed between the advancing Allies.

☐ Maximum extent of Axis Powers, Nov. 1942

☐ Neutral states

➤ Soviet advances

☐ Unoccupied Allied Powers

➤ Allied advances

Battle of Britain

Journalists called the period up to spring 1940 the "phoney war," because Britain and France did little fighting. In August, Göring's Luftwaffe (air force) started trying to destroy the British RAF (Royal Air Force). Hitler's idea was to follow this with an invasion of Britain. Despite being outnumbered and losing about 900 planes, the RAF destroyed about 1,700 German aircraft and won the battle. Hitler changed his plans in October 1940 and turned to bombing British cities.

General Montgomery in the desert in North Africa.

North African Campaigns

During 1940, British troops fought the Italians in North Africa for control of Egypt, the Suez Canal and routes to the oil fields of the Middle East. In 1941, Hitler sent over tank divisions led by Field Marshal Erwin Rommel, known as the "Desert Fox." Rommel came up against the British commander Bernard Montgomery, who stopped the German advance at the Egyptian port of El Alamein. The Allies used their strength in North Africa to invade Sicily, southern Italy, in July 1943.

Operation Barbarossa

Germany and the Soviet Union were uneasy, distrustful partners. Before the end of 1940, Hitler drafted plans to invade Russia, code-naming the secret operation Barbarossa. The unexpected attack began in June 1941 and at first was successful, but the Russians showed great resistance in the siege of Leningrad. In the winter of 1942–43, German troops were beaten by Soviet forces and freezing temperatures at Stalingrad, and were forced to surrender.

German tanks were successful in the early months of the campaign on the Eastern Front. But the starving German troops (below) were finally defeated.

Britain's Home Front

British civilians were prepared for war as soon as it was declared. A blackout was introduced, evacuation was ordered and air-raid routines become the norm. In London and other major cities, bombing took a heavy toll, and by May 1941 more than 43,000 civilians had been killed. While men were away in the armed services, women took their place in farms and factories.

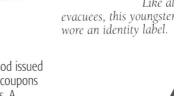

The Germans called the V-2 liquid-fuel rocket a "vengeance weapon."

Evacuation

At the outbreak of war, children, and pregnant women were evacuated from cities in danger of German bombing, such as London, Birmingham, and Portsmouth. Evacuees went by train to live with civilians in country villages. Nearly two million children were evacuated in the first few weeks, but many returned home before bombing started in earnest. Mothers found the split-up of their families very hard to bear. Altogether 3.5 million people were evacuated in Britain during the war.

Like all evacuees, this youngster wore an identity label.

Rationing

The Ministry of Food issued ration books with coupons for restricted foods. A weekly ration allowed small amounts of bacon, butter, cheese, lard, margarine, meat, sugar, and tea. In addition, a person could have up to 8 ounces of jam and a packet of dried egg every month, plus an egg every fortnight. Children were allowed daily orange juice and cod liver oil, and infants got an extra allowance of milk.

Families got used to the routine of going into their shelter when they heard an air-raid siren.

Air-raid Shelters

Public air-raid shelters were built in schools and parks, most holding about 100 people. In London, people sheltered in underground railway stations. At home, families with gardens were issued with corrugated-iron Anderson shelters that could be half-buried under earth. Indoors, people put rigid-steel cages (Morrison shelters) under tables. Curtains with black linings "blacked out" all windows after dark, so that German planes could not spot targets.

A 1941 ration book. There were spaces to enter the names of approved shops.

A Home Guard volunteer stands on a London rooftop on the lookout for enemy planes.

The Home Guard

Local Defense Volunteers guarded against parachute landings by German troops. In June 1940, the force changed its name to the Home Guard. Most volunteers were too young or too old to serve in the armed forces. They were issued with a basic uniform, tin hat and rifle, and by 1943 the force numbered about two million. At the same time, more than one million women joined the Women's Voluntary Service (WVS).

Helping the War Effort

One of the most successful slogans of the war was "Dig for victory." This was part of a programme to get people to turn their gardens into mini-allotments and grow their own food. Housewives were also encouraged to "make do and mend," recycling and repairing their clothing, especially after clothes rationing was introduced in 1941. Metal was collected for recycling in factories.

WVS volunteers collected pots, pans and even old railings, for use in munitions factories.

Inspection of St John Ambulance volunteers in 1939.

Women's Work

Women were needed to take on essential jobs. One advertising slogan read, "For a healthy happy job, join the Women's Land Army." Volunteers worked on farms to keep agriculture going. Other women worked in munitions factories, and some became mechanics, plumbers, fire-engine or ambulance drivers. Many took on night jobs, and nurseries were set up to provide childcare by day.

The Blitz

On September 7, 1940, 348 German bombers attacked East London. This was the start of the Blitz, a series of 127 large-scale air raids on London and other cities over a period of nine months. People spent most nights in their shelters. There were 71 raids on London alone, in which 20,000 people were killed and 1.4 million made homeless. Barrage balloons were put up to stop low-flying aircraft and force the bombers higher.

London's St Paul's Cathedral was surrounded by fire but suffered little damage.

Air-raid damage in Battersea, to the south of London, in 1940.

BRITAIN'S HOME FRONT

1939
The Military Training Act calls for all British men aged 20–21 to do military service. Identity cards are introduced.

1940
Food rationing is introduced. The Local Defense Volunteers force is created, as proposed by War Minister Anthony Eden.

1941
Conscription is introduced for all men aged 18–50, except those in reserved occupations, and for unmarried women aged 20–30 (for non-fighting service).

1942
In April, heavy bombing raids are made on Bath, Exeter, Norwich and York in retaliation for raids on Germany.

1944
So-called "Baby Blitz" bombings on London and southern England; on June 13, the first V-1 "doodlebug" flying bomb hits Hackney, East London; on Sep 8, the first V-2 rocket hits London.

1945
The Family Allowances Act gives mothers a tax-free cash payment for each of their children.

Many people lost all their possessions in the conflict, as well as their homes.

Battle for the Pacific

EXTRA *Los Angeles Times* **NIGHT Pictorial**

IT'S WAR!
Hostilities Declared by Japanese; 350 Reported Killed in Hawaii Raid
U.S. Battleships Hit, 7 Die in Honolulu
Air Bombs Rained on Pacific Bases

A US front-page report on Pearl Harbor (above). Many Japanese-Americans were immediately put into makeshift US resettlement camps.

In an effort to discourage Japanese expansion by force into China and French Indo-China, a number of western powers stopped selling oil, iron ore and steel to Japan. Japan saw this embargo as an act of aggression and responded by attacking the US fleet at Pearl Harbor. The attack immediately brought the United States into the war, and Japanese territorial gains were short-lived.

This poster shows Japanese tentacles grasping Southeast Asia, including the Dutch East Indies. It reads: "The Indies must be free! Work and fight for it!"

INDIE MOET VRIJ !
WERKT EN VECHT ERVOOR !

Japanese Conquests

In 1942, Japanese forces swept across much of Southeast Asia, including Burma, Malaya, the Philippines, the Dutch East Indies, northern New Guinea, and the Solomon Islands. Following the lightning capture of Malaya, three Japanese divisions took the British stronghold of Singapore island in a week. Prime Minister Winston Churchill described this loss as the "greatest disaster and capitulation in British history."

POWs at Japanese camps were kept on starvation rations. Japanese commanders took the view that captives had dishonored their country.

Prisoners of War

The fall of Singapore to Japan led to many thousands of Allied servicemen being captured. Many were taken to a prisoner-of-war camp at Changi, in the east of the island. Conditions there were brutally harsh. Inmates were used as forced labour and only those strong enough to work were fed properly. There was poor medical treatment, and one in three prisoners of war died in Japanese camps.

Struggle for Naval Supremacy

The USA had an important base at Midway Island, to the northwest of Hawaii. When a Japanese fleet approached the island atoll in June 1942, US planes responded at once. They sank four Japanese aircraft carriers and one cruiser, destroying more than 200 planes. This was a decisive victory for the Americans. It crippled Japan's naval air power and was a turning point in the overall battle for control of the Pacific.

In the later years of the war, Japan used kamikaze suicide pilots, who flew aircraft packed with explosives into target ships.

BATTLE FOR THE PACIFIC

1941
On December 7, the Japanese attack Pearl Harbor, on the Hawaiian island of Oahu; the next day, the US and Britain declare war on Japan; on December 11, the US declares war on Germany and Italy.

1942
In February, Japan captures Singapore and wins the Battle of the Java Sea; in April, US bombers attack Tokyo; in May, in the Battle of the Coral Sea, the US lose ships, but stop Japanese expansion.

1943
In February, British-Indian forces wage jungle warfare against the Japanese in Burma; in October, Emperor Hirohito calls Japan's situation "truly grave"; in November, US forces invade the Gilbert Islands, with heavy losses.

1944
In June, the US wins the Battle of the Philippine Sea; in July, the worsening situation forces Japanese prime minister Hideki Tojo to resign; in October, Allied forces land in the Philippines.

1945
In March, US marines capture Iwo Jima; in June, Allied forces capture the Japanese island of Okinawa.

US marines storm ashore from their landing craft at Guadalcanal. The battle for the island lasted 6 months and ended in an Allied victory.

Island Battles

US marines fought famous battles to take Japanese-held islands. In 1942, they invaded Guadalcanal in the Solomon Islands. This was followed by a successful island-hopping campaign. By early 1945, the Americans were ready to invade Iwo Jima, a tiny island 745 miles (1,200 km) south of Japan, defended by Japanese troops in fortified caves and tunnels. The fighting lasted almost a month. The US victory allowed them to use the island as a base against Japan.

This still from the 2001 film Pearl Harbor *shows a Japanese dive-bomber flying over damaged US ships.*

WAR IN THE PACIFIC AND FAR EAST, 1941–45

USSR
MANCHURIA
CHINA
JAPAN
•HIROSHIMA
NAGASAKI
IWO JIMA
MIDWAY ISLANDS
INDIA
BURMA
HONG KONG
HAWAIIAN ISLANDS
MARSHALL ISLANDS
MALAYA
SINGAPORE
PHILIPPINES
DUTCH EAST INDIES
GUADALCANAL
AUSTRALIA

- ■ Maximum area occupied by Japan 1942
- → Allied advances
- → Soviet advances

Gains and Losses

Following Pearl Harbor, the Japanese expanded their empire. They captured the mainland of Southeast Asia (including the important British crown colony of Hong Kong) and the Pacific islands. From mid-1942, the US and their Allies slowly regained this territory, but with enormous loss of life on both sides.

Pearl Harbor

The Japanese surprise air attack on the US naval base in Hawaii came without any previous declaration of war. Japanese aircraft carriers launched 350 planes to attack the US fleet, and the attack lasted just two hours. The Japanese destroyed or damaged 21 American ships, including 8 battleships, and more than 300 planes, killing more than 2,300 people. President Roosevelt called December 7 "a date which will live in infamy."

Path to Victory

In June 1944, Allied forces landed on the north coast of France and began the liberation of Europe. At the same time, the Russians pushed the German army back on the Eastern Front. Having lost Italy to the south, Germany had effectively lost the war, but Hitler refused to accept this until April 1945. After finally gaining victory in Europe, the Allies used the world's first atomic bombs to force Japan's surrender and end the World War.

On June 6 1944 (D-Day), Allied troops landed on the coast of German-occupied Normandy, France.

D-Day

The Germans expected the Allies to invade France near Cala the narrowest point of the English Channel. But Normandy, further west, was chosen for Operation Overlord. On D-Day US, British and Canadian troops took the Germans by surp as they landed on the beaches. They were backed by nava bombardments and air attacks. By the end of the month, about a million Allied soldiers had reached France and were gradually fighting their way south.

Operation Bagration

Towards the end of June 1944, the Russians launched a massive four-prong offensive against the Germans' Eastern Front. Stalin code-named the operation Bagration, after a great Russian general of the Napoleonic Wars. In four weeks, the huge Soviet army re-conquered Byelorussia (Belarus), destroying thousands of tanks and inflicting huge losses on the German army. Hitler's forces were now being squeezed from both west and east.

A Soviet infantry scout with his well-trained dog.

US and Free French forces liberated Paris on 25 August 1944. Hitler had ordered his commanders to destroy the city, but instead they surrendered.

The End of Hitler

By the end of 1944, the war was going disastrously for Germany. But Hitler still refused to give in. In his bunker beneath Berlin, the Nazi leader still seemed to believe the hopeless situation could be turned around. When Soviet troops entered the capital, Hitler at last accepted the truth. On 30 April, in his underground bunker, he finally killed himself; his body was burned by one of his personal guards. The Nazi regime was at an end.

HITLER DEAD

The front page of a British newspaper, 2 May 1945, tells of Hitler's death.

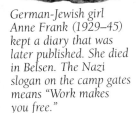

German-Jewish girl Anne Frank (1929–45) kept a diary that was later published. She died in Belsen. The Nazi slogan on the camp gates means "Work makes you free."

The Holocaust

The Holocaust (meaning "complete destruction by fire") is the name given to the mass murder of Jews by the Nazis. Many millions of Jewish people—men, women and children—were sent to concentration camps. They were starved, tortured, and forced to work. Many were murdered in gas chambers and their bodies incinerated, in death camps such as Auschwitz and Belsen. About six million Jews died in the Holocaust.

The "Big Three" leaders, Winston Churchill (UK), Franklin D. Roosevelt (USA) and Joseph Stalin (USSR).

Yalta Conference

In February 1945, Allied leaders Churchill, Roosevelt and Stalin–representing the "Big Three" nations–met at Yalta, in the Crimea. They discussed strategy for finishing the war, the proposed occupation of Germany and its division into four zones. The leaders also agreed to the formation of a new peacekeeping organization (the United Nations).

Victory in Europe

May 8, 1945, the day after the full German surrender, was called VE (for Victory in Europe) Day. Churchill appeared with King George VI and his family on the balcony of Buckingham Palace in London, waving to enormous, cheering crowds. Churchill said, "In all our long history we have never seen a greater day than this." In the United States, President Harry Truman dedicated victory to the memory of President Roosevelt, who had died only a few weeks earlier.

President Truman said: "We have used [the atomic bomb] to shorten the agony of war."

Victory over Japan

In 1945, US bombers increased their raids on Japan. On August 6 and 9, they dropped atomic bombs on the cities of Hiroshima and Nagasaki. The bombs killed at least 110,000 people immediately, and many thousands more later from burns and radiation. On September 2, Japan formally surrendered.

A watch found at Hiroshima, showing the time of the blast, 8:15 in the morning.

PATH TO VICTORY

1944
On July 20, a bomb plot to assassinate Hitler is unsuccessful, and leading conspirator Colonel Claus von Stauffenberg is executed. On September 4, Antwerp and Brussels are liberated by the Allies.

1945
*In March, US incendiary bombs destroy central Tokyo.
On April 25, Dachau concentration camp is liberated.
On May 2nd, German troops in Italy surrender.
May 7 sees the unconditional surrender of all German forces. The following day is VE (Victory in Europe) Day. On May 23, Heinrich Himmler (head of the SS) commits suicide. The Potsdam Conference declaration (July 26) demands that Japan surrender or face "utter destruction." August 15 is VJ (Victory over Japan) Day (also celebrated on Sept. 2, the day of formal surrender).*

In Britain there were huge celebrations on VE Day, with singing, dancing and parties in the streets.

Arts and Science

Between the two world wars, all forms of art moved toward becoming more personal and emotional. Yet at the same time painting and other forms tended towards the abstract, as artists allowed themselves more freedom of expression. In science, there were great medical and technological breakthroughs. One of the greatest was in nuclear physics, which led inevitably—and unfortunately, according to many—to the creation of the first atomic weapons.

Illumined Pleasures by Salvador Dalí (1904–89), painted in 1929, can be interpreted as a dream sequence.

An Art Deco jar of the 1920s.

Virginia Woolf (1882–1941) was a central figure in the Bloomsbury Group. Two of her most famous novels were Mrs Dalloway *(1925) and* To the Lighthouse *(1927).*

New Art Movements

Surrealism began as a literary movement in France in the 1920s. During the following decades many artists reflected in their paintings the irrational forces of dreams and the subconscious. Famous surrealists were Salvador Dalí, Max Ernst, René Magritte, and Joan Miró. Another movement, called Art Deco ("decorative art"), emphasized bold shapes and colors in design and architecture.

Literary Groups

In the Bloomsbury district of London, a group of writers and intellectuals opposed the conservative nature of English society in their lives and work. They included writers E.M. Forster and Virginia Woolf, philosopher Bertrand Russell, and economist John Maynard Keynes. In Paris, a group of exiled Americans made up the "Lost Generation." Writers such as F. Scott Fitzgerald, Ernest Hemingway, and Ezra Pound had lost faith in the materialist society of the post-war United States.

Manhattan Project

The Americans feared that German scientists might, like them, be working on an atomic bomb. A top-secret project code-named Manhattan was set up in 1942, with laboratories and other facilities in New Mexico, Tennessee and Washington. Physicist J. Robert Oppenheimer was in charge of designing and building an atomic bomb. The first one was successfully tested in New Mexico in July 1945.

Soaring Architecture

Skyscrapers reflected Art Deco style, as new materials and building methods allowed them to grow ever taller. The tallest of all was the Empire State Building in New York, which stood as the world's tallest building for more than forty years.

Chrysler Building, New York, 1930, 319 m (1,046 ft).

GE Building, New York, 1933, 259 m (849 ft).

Empire State Building, New York, 1931, 381 m (1,250 ft).

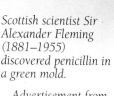

Scottish scientist Sir Alexander Fleming (1881–1955) discovered penicillin in a green mold.

Advertisement from Woman and Home magazine for nylon stockings ("nylons").

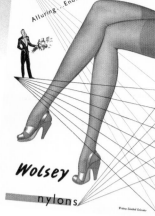

Nylon
In 1935, Wallace H. Carothers, a chemist working for the DuPont Company, created a new synthetic fiber called polyhexamethylene adipamide. Four years later, the first products were being made of this new material—given the simpler name of nylon—including parachutes. After the war, its most popular use was as ladies' stockings.

Antibiotics
The first antibiotic was discovered in 1928 and named penicillin after the mold in which it was found. By 1941 scientists had found ways of using penicillin to treat infections in humans by killing harmful bacteria. This was an enormous step forward in medicine.

Jacques-Yves Cousteau (1910–97) (above) also invented a way of using television underwater.

Undersea World
In 1943, the French oceanographer Jacques-Yves Cousteau and engineer Emile Gagnan invented a breathing device called the aqualung. This allowed divers to stay underwater for long periods. Two years later Cousteau founded the French navy's Office of Undersea Research at Marseilles. His invention was useful both for locating and removing enemy mines and, after the war, for the exploration of marine life.

The uranium bomb dropped on Hiroshima (see page 43) was code-named Little Boy.

The 102-storey Empire State Building was constructed by a workforce of 3,500 in just over a year. It was made of steel, aluminim, limestone and 10 million bricks.

Grand Rex Cinema, Paris, 1932, the largest film theatre in Europe.

(see page 43)

ARTS AND SCIENCE

1924
The Surrealist Manifesto is published by French poet André Breton (1896–1966).

1925
An International Exposition of Modern Industrial and Decorative Arts is held in Paris (creating the term Art Deco).

1926
Ernest Hemingway (1899–1961) uses Gertrude Stein's phrase "You are all a lost generation" in the preface to The Sun Also Rises.

1931
Eugene O'Neill's Mourning Becomes Electra is performed in New York.

1932
Aldous Huxley's futuristic Brave New World is published.

1933
The German school of design called the Bauhaus, founded by Walter Gropius (1883–1969), is closed down by the Nazis.

1935
Scottish engineer Robert Watson-Watt first uses radar to detect aircraft.

1937
First aero jet engine tested.

1942
US physicist Enrico Fermi (1901–54) produces the first successful nuclear chain reaction.

1943
The huge computer Colossus helps the British break German codes.

1945
Alexander Fleming shares the Nobel Prize for Medicine for discovering penicillin.

Glossary

Abdication To abdicate is to give up one's responsibilities. King Edward VILI abdicated as king when told that the twice-divorced Mrs Simpson would not be accepted as queen if he married her.

Appease To calm someone down by giving in to their demands. Chamberlain tried to appease Hitler during the Munich crisis of 1938.

Atoll A ring-shaped coral reef.

Axis Powers
The Fascist allies fighting on Germany's side in World War II. Hitler and Mussolini in 1936 had talked about "a Rome–Berlin axis round which all European states can assemble." Japan joined the Axis in 1936, Hungary, Romania and Bulgaria during the war.

"Beer hall putsch" A rising staged by Hitler and the Nazi party in 1923 in Munich. It failed and Hitler was sent to prison.

Bolshevik In Russian, "a member of the majority." Bolsheviks were followers of Lenin, who in 1918 changed their name to the Russian Communist Party.

Bootleg liquor Alcohol illegally sold during Prohibition. The term refers to bottles secretly carried in the leg of someone's boot.

Boycott To boycott someone is to have nothing further to do with that person; if a meeting is boycotted, nobody attends it. The word comes from a Captain Boycott in 19th-century Ireland, whose tenants refused to work for him after he threw some of them out of their homes for not paying rent.

Cinematic technique The art of using all the special skills needed to make a film–direction, photography, editing, lighting etc.–in the most memorable way.

Commissar The head of a government department in the Soviet Union.

Constitutional Crisis Refers to the Abdication of King Edward VILI from the British throne. No other British king had decided of his own accord to give up the crown, so there were no rules in place to guide the government as to how to handle the situation.

Court of International Justice A body (established in 1921) that set out the rules that states consider legally binding when they deal with each other. Replaced in 1946 by the International Court of Justice that meets at the Hague, in the Netherlands.

Depression A time of world economic crisis, particularly the Great Depression of the 1930s, when a slump in the value of stocks caused people to panic and withdraw their money from banks, forcing them to close. Shops and businesses could not function and millions lost their jobs.

Falange From the Spanish for "phalanx"–a line of troops ready to fight. The name of the Fascist Party in Spain in the 1930s.

Fascism A political belief holding that people should obey the will of the state, which itself should be controlled by a strong leader. Mussolini, Hitler and Franco were all Fascists. The movement arose to fight communism, but used many similar ways to influence people.

Gestapo The Nazi secret police (Geheime Staatspolizei). In 1939, it merged with the Security Service (SD), the intelligence branch of the SS. It had powers to torture and execute anyone suspected of working against the Nazis.

Gulag A labour camp in the USSR. Gulags were set up by Stalin in remote areas such as Siberia to house thousands of political prisoners, who were brutally treated.

Indian National Congress The main political party in India. It led the campaign for independence from British rule.

International Labor Organization An agency founded in 1919 to improve standards in work and living throughout the world.

Kamikaze Japanese for "divine wind," this was the name given to a plane loaded with explosives that was deliberately crashed into an enemy ship. The pilot had no hope of survival.

Lateran Treaties Agreements signed in 1929 (in the Lateran Palace in Rome) between the kingdom of Italy and the Pope, creating a new papal state, Vatican City, fully independent of Italian control.

Mandate An order from the League of Nations to a country, giving it power to administer another country or territory (large piece of land).

Nationalists Members of a political party who believe that the country to which they belong should be or become independent.

Newspaper magnate The influential owner of many of a country's newspapers, in a position to decide what the papers will say about a topic.

Oceanographer Someone who studies the seas: their climates and everything that lives in them.

"Phoney war" The word "phoney" was 1930s American slang for "false, fake." From the outbreak of war until spring 1940, little seemed to happen.

Pocket battleship Battleships are naval vessels that carry the heaviest armour and the largest guns. Pocket battleships are slightly smaller, but still immensely powerful.

Propaganda Information, often one-sided or untrue, given out by a government or party to influence people in their favor, particularly through articles, radio broadcasts, and films.

Reparations Compensation paid by a losing side in a war for the damage it caused to the land and population of the winning side.

Reserved occupations Jobs so important to the country's welfare that people who held them were not called up for the Forces with others of their age-group.

Slump A sudden heavy and serious fall in the value of a country's economy, when business and the stock market are affected and people are thrown out of work.

Soviet In Russian, originally "a council of workers' delegates." Refers to the Union of Soviet Socialist Republics, a Communist state in eastern Europe and northern Asia made up of Russia and 14 republics.

Speakeasy A club where alcohol could illegally be obtained during Prohibition. The term refers to asking for the drink "easy," that is "quietly," for fear of being overheard.

Speculate To invest money in stocks and shares in the hope of making a lot more money as they increase in value and can be sold at a profit.

SS The elite unit of the German Nazi Party, founded by Hitler to be his personal bodyguard. The Gestapo was a division of the SS; the Waffen-SS administered the concentration camps.

Stock Exchange A "market" where securities (documents that give the buyer the right to receive interest or dividends from the money invested) can be bought and sold.

Subconscious The area of people's thought that lies in the mind below the thoughts of which they are fully aware. Subconscious thoughts may surface in dreams.

Surrealism A movement in art and literature from the 1920s on that abandoned reason and logic in favor of strange, dreamlike images.

Synagogue A Jewish place of worship.

Index

Abyssinia (now Ethiopia) 22, 23
Admiral Graf Spee (battleship) 36
agriculture 12, 14, 15, 20, 21, 23, 39
air mail 10
air raids 35, 38, 39
Albania 22, 23
Alcock, John 10
Alfonso XIII (King of Spain) 30
Allies 6, 23, 35, 36, 37, 40–41, 42–43
Anschluss 34, 35
antibiotics (penicillin) 44
architecture 44, 45
Art Deco 44, 45
arts 44–45
atomic bomb/weapons 5, 42, 43, 44, 45
Australia 7, 11, 27, 35, 41
Austria/Austrian 32, 33, 34, 35
Austria-Hungary 7
Axis Powers 36, 37

Baldwin, Stanley (Prime Minister of Britain) 27
barrage balloons 39
baseball 9
– Ruth, George Herman ("Babe") 9
battles
– Atlantic, Battle of the 36, 37
– "Battle for grain" (Italy) 23
– "Battle for land" (Italy) 23
– Britain, Battle of 36
– Coral Sea, Battle of the 40
– El Alamein, Battle of 37
– Guadalcanal 41
– Java Sea, Battle of the 40
– Pacific, Battle for the 40–41
– Philippine Sea, Battle of the 40
– Spanish Civil War 30
– Stalingrad, Battle of 37
Bauhaus school of design 45
Belarus 18, 19, 42
Birdseye, Clarence 9
Bismarck (battleship) 36
blackout 38
Blackshirts 22, 23
Blitz 39
Bloomsbury Group 4, 44
Bolsheviks 18, 19, 20, 21
Bonnie and Clyde (Parker, Bonnie and Barrow, Clyde) 12
books and plays 44–45
– *Brave New World*, Aldous

Huxley 45
– *Grapes of Wrath, The*, John Steinbeck 14, 15
– *Homage to Catalonia*, George Orwell 31
– Mein Kampf *("My Struggle")*, Adolf Hitler 33
– *Mourning Becomes Electra*, Eugene O'Neill 45
– *Mrs Dalloway*, Virginia Woolf 44
– *Surrealist Manifesto*, André Breton 45
– *The Sun Also Rises*, Ernest Hemingway 45
– *To the Lighthouse*, Virginia Woolf 44
Breton, André 45
Britain (UK)/British 4, 5, 7, 10, 12, 13, 18, 23, 24, 25, 26–27, 30, 31, 34, 35, 36, 37, 38–39, 40, 42, 43, 45
– British Empire 7, 26, 27
Brownshirts 32, 33
Buick Motor Company 10
Buñuel, Luis 31
Burma 40
Byelorussia (now Belarus) 42

Canada 4, 10, 27
Capone, Al 8, 9
Carothers, Wallace H. 45
Chamberlain, Neville (Prime Minister of Britain) 34
Chiang Kai-shek (Jiang Jieshi) 28, 29
China/Chinese 4, 5, 28–29, 40
– civil war 28
– Long March 28
Church (Roman Catholic) 30, 33
Churchill, Winston 26, 36, 40, 43
Civilian Conservation Corps (CCC) 14, 15
civilians 5, 30, 38
Clemenceau, Georges (Prime Minister of France) 6
Colossus (computer) 45
Commonwealth of Nations 5, 26, 27
Communism/Communists 4, 5, 7, 18, 19, 20, 21, 22, 28, 29, 30, 31, 33
concentration camps 42,43
conscription 5, 39
Cousteau, Jacques-Yves 45
Czechoslovakia 5, 7, 33, 34, 35

Daladier, Edouard (Prime Minister of France) 34
Dalí, Salvador 31, 44
D-Day 37, 42
Denmark 37
Disney, Walt/Disney Studio 9, 16, 17
Dust Bowl 12

Eastern Front 37, 42
Eden, Anthony (British War Minister) 39
Edward VILI (King of England) 5, 7, 27
Egypt 25, 37
El Alamein 37
Empire State Building, New York 13, 17, 44, 45
Eritrea 23
Ernst, Max 44
Ethiopia 22, 23
evacuation 38

Faisal I (Emir then King of Iraq) 24, 25
famine, in Russia 4, 5, 21
Fascism/Fascists 4, 5, 6, 7, 17, 22–23, 30
Fermi, Enrico 45
film actors/directors 9, 14, 16, 17
– Barrymore, John 16
– Chaplin, Charlie 16, 17
– Cooper, Gary 17
– Dietrich, Marlene 17, 23
– Fairbanks, Douglas Sr 16, 17
– Fields, W.C. 17
– Ford, John 14, 17
– Hitchcock, Alfred 17
– Huston, Walter 17
– Jolson, Al 9, 16
– Pickford, Mary 16
– Valentino, Rudolph 4, 16, 17
– Wayne, John 17
– Welles, Orson 16, 17
films 9, 14, 16–17, 33, 41
– *Citizen Kane* 16, 17
– *Don Juan* 16
– *Flowers and Trees* 16
– *Four Horsemen of the Apocalypse, The* 4, 17
– *Gold Rush, The* 17
– *Gone with the Wind* 17
– *Grapes of Wrath, The* 14
– *Great Dictator, The* 17

– *Hunchback of Notre Dame, The* 17
– *Jazz Singer, The* 9, 16
– *King Kong* 17
– *Pearl Harbor* 41
– *Rebecca* 17
– *Robin Hood* 17
– *Sheik, The* 16
– *Snow White and the Seven Dwarfs* 17
– *Son of the Sheik* 16
– *Stagecoach* 17
– *Steamboat Willie* 9
– *Virginian, The* 17
– *Wizard of Oz, The* 17
Finland 18, 35
Fitzgerald, F. Scott 44
Fleming, Sir Alexander 44, 45
Ford, Henry 10
Forster, E.M. 44
Fourth International 5, 21
France/French 5, 6, 7, 18, 23, 24, 25, 27, 30, 31, 32, 33, 34, 35, 36, 37, 42, 44
Franco, Francisco (El Caudillo) 5, 7, 22, 30, 31
Frank, Anne 42

Gagnan, Emile 45
Gandhi, Mohandas 27
General Strike 26
George V (King of England) 5, 26, 27
George VI (King of England) 5, 27, 43
Germany/Germans 4, 5, 6, 7, 12, 13, 18, 19, 22, 23, 25, 30, 31, 32–33, 34, 35, 36–37, 39, 40, 42, 43, 45
Gestapo 33
Goebbels, Joseph (German Propaganda Minister) 34
Göring, Hermann Wilhelm 33, 36
Great Depression 12–13, 14, 17
Great Purge 21
Greece 37
Gropius, Walter 45

Haile Selassie (Emperor of Abyssinia) 22
Hemingway, Ernest 31, 44, 45
Hideki Tojo (Prime Minister of Japan) 40
Himmler, Heinrich (head of the SS)

43
Hindenburg, Paul von (President of Germany) 32, 33
Hirohito (Emperor of Japan) 40
Hiroshima, Japan 43, 45
Hitler, Adolf (*Der Führer*) 4, 5, 7, 22, 31, 32–33, 34, 35, 36–37, 42,43
Hollywood 16–17, 33
Holocaust 42
Home Guard 38
Hoover, Herbert (President of USA) 13
Huxley, Aldous 45

India/Indian 26, 27, 40
industry 9, 11, 14, 20, 21, 22, 26
Ireland/Irish 4, 10, 26, 27
Italy/Italians 4, 5, 6, 7, 22–23, 25, 30, 34, 36, 37, 40, 42, 43
Izvestia (newspaper) 19

Japan/Japanese 5, 7, 18, 22, 23, 28, 29, 34, 40–41, 42, 43
Japanese-Americans 40
jazz 9
Jews/Jewish 8, 24, 25, 33, 34, 42

kamikaze suicide pilots 40
Keynes, John Maynard 44
Kingdom of Serbs, Croats and Slovenes 7
Kirov, Sergey 21
Kristallnacht 34
Ku Klux Klan 8

League of Nations 5, 7, 8, 22, 24, 34, 35
Lenin (Vladimir Ilyich Ulyanov) 4, 18, 19, 20, 21
Leningrad, siege of 37
Lindbergh, Charles 10, 11
Lloyd George, David (Prime Minister of Britain) 6
Lorca, Federico Garcia 31
Luftwaffe (German air force) 36

Magritte, René 44
Malaya (now Malaysia) 40, 41
Manhattan Project 45
Mao Zeroing 4, 5, 28, 29
Messerschmitt (fighter plane) 36
Middle East 4, 5, 7, 24–25, 37
Midway Island 40
Miró, Joan 30, 44
Molotov, Vyacheslav (Foreign Minister of the Soviet Union) 37

Montgomery, Bernard Law (Field Marshal) 37
Moran, Bugs 9
Munich Agreement 34
music and songs 8, 9, 10, 13, 16
Muslim League 27
Mussolini, Benito (*Il Duce*) 4, 5, 7, 22, 23, 34

Nagasaki, Japan 41, 43
National Socialist German Workers' (Nazi) Party 32, 33
Nazi Germany 5, 25, 30, 32, 33, 34, 35, 36, 42, 45
Nazi-Soviet Pact 37
Netherlands 37
New Deal (USA) 5, 14–15
New Economic Policy (Russia) 19
New York Stock Exchange 4, 12, 13
New Zealand 7, 27, 35
Night of the Long Knives 32
North Africa 36, 37
Norway 37
nuclear physics 44, 45

O'Neill, Eugene 45
Operation Bagration 42
Operation Barbarossa 37
Operation Overlord 42
Oppenheimer, J. Robert 45
Orlando, Vittorio (Prime Minister of Italy) 6
Orwell, George 31
Ottoman Empire 7, 24, 25
Owens, Jesse 33

Pact of Steel 5, 23
Palestine/Palestinians 4, 5, 24, 25
Pearl Harbor 5, 40, 41
Persia (now Iran) 4, 24
"phoney war" 36
Picasso, Pablo 31
Pilsudski, Jozef (Polish leader) 19
Pius XI, Pope 23
Poland 5, 7, 18, 34, 35, 37
Potsdam Conference 43
Pound, Ezra 44
Prohibition 8, 9, 13
Prussia, East 7

racism 8, 33
radar 45
radio 9, 10
RAF (Royal Air Force) 25, 36
rationing 38, 39, 40
Red Army 18, 19

Ribbentrop, Joachim von (Foreign Minister of Germany) 37
Röhm, Ernst (SA leader) 32
Romania 35
Rome–Berlin Axis 22, 23
Rommel, Erwin (Field Marshal) 37
Roosevelt, Franklin Delano (President of USA) 5, 14, 15, 41, 43
Russell, Bertrand 44
Russia/Russian 4, 5, 18, 19, 20–21, 35, 37, 42
Russian Civil War 18
Russo-Polish War 19

SA (Sturmabteilung) 32, 33
Salt March 27
Saudi Arabia 5, 25
Schleicher, Kurt von (German Chancellor) 32
Schuschnigg, Kurt von (Austrian Chancellor) 35
science 44–45
Securities Exchange Commission 14
Simpson, Mrs Wallis 27
Singapore 40, 41
Sino-Japanese War 29
Somaliland (Somalia) 23
Soviet Union 4, 5, 7, 18–19, 20–21, 23, 29, 30, 31, 34, 35, 36, 37
– collectivization 20, 21
– Five Year Plans 21
– gulags (labor camps) 20
Spain/Spanish 4, 5, 7, 30–31
– Civil War 30, 31
speakeasies 8
Spirit of St. Louis (airplane) 11
Spitfire fighter plane 36
SS (Schutzstaffel) 32, 33, 43
Stakhanov, Alexei 20
Stalin, Joseph (Iosif Dzhugashvili) 4, 5, 7, 19, 20–21, 36, 37, 42, 43
Stalingrad 37
Stauffenberg, Claus von (Colonel) 43
Stein, Gertrude 45
Steinbeck, John 14
Sudetenland 34, 35
Suez Canal 37
Sun Yat-sen 4, 29
Surrealism 31, 44, 45
Third International 19
Third Reich 7, 33, 34, 35
Trades Union Congress 26
Transcaucasia (now Azerbaijan, Armenia and Georgia) 18
transport 10–11, 18, 38

Treaty of Brest–Litovsk 19
Treaty of Versailles 5, 6, 7, 8
Trotsky, Leon 4, 5, 18, 19, 20, 21
Truman, Harry S. (President of USA) 43
Turkey 4, 23, 24
Turkmenistan 19

U-boats 36, 37
Ukraine 18, 19, 21
United Nations 43
United States of America/Americans 4, 5, 8–9, 10–11, 12–13, 14–15, 16–17, 27, 30, 31, 33, 36, 37, 40, 41, 43, 44, 45
Uruguay 36
Uzbekistan 19

V-1 "doodlebug" flying bomb 39
V-2 liquid-fuel rocket 38, 39
Vatican, the 31
VE (Victory in Europe) Day 43
Victor Emmanuel III (King of Italy) 22
Vishinsky, Andrey 21
VJ (Victory over Japan) Day 43

Wall Street Crash (Black Thursday) 13
Watson-Watt, Robert 45
Weimar Republic 33
Whitten Brown, Arthur 10
Wilson, Woodrow (President of USA) 6
Women's Land Army 39
Women's Voluntary Service (WVS) 38, 39
Woolf, Virginia 4, 44
World War I (Great War) 5, 6, 8, 19, 24, 26, 32
World War II 4, 5, 14, 22, 23, 31, 34–35, 36–37, 38–39, 40–41, 42–43

Yalta Conference 43
Yugoslavia 37

Zamora, Niceto Alcalá 31
Zinoviev, Grigori 21